NIGERIAN GENOCIDE: CHRISTIAN PERSECUTION 2014

Laura Murray

Print Edition

Copyright 2015 Laura Murray

Table of Contents

INTRODUCTION 5

NIGERIA 7
HISTORY (CONDENSED) 7
SYMBOLS 9
ETHNIC, RELIGIOUS, AND OTHER IDENTITIES 10
GOVERNMENT, ECONOMY, MILITARY, & CRIME 12
DISCUSSION QUESTIONS 15

HAUSA-FULANI 17
HAUSA TRIBE 18
FULANI TRIBE 18
HAUSA-FULANI POLITICS 20
FULANI AND CHRISTIANS 23
NEWS STORIES & WITNESS ACCOUNTS 27
FULANI AND BOKO HARAM 32
FULANI & GENOCIDE 35
CONCLUSION 38
QUESTIONS 38

BOKO HARAM 41
HISTORY 41
LEADERSHIP 44
CONNECTIONS, AID, & FINANCING 47
TACTICS 52
BOKO HARAM & CHRISTIANS 56
NEWS STORIES & WITNESS ACCOUNTS 63
BOKO HARAM'S CALIPHATE 83
BOKO HARAM & GENOCIDE 84
CONCLUSION 86
DISCUSSION QUESTIONS 86

BRING BACK OUR GIRLS ... 89
CASE ... 90
TIMELINE ... 90
WHAT HAPPENED? ... 94
WHAT IS BEING DONE? ... 95
WHAT IS BOKO HARAM DOING WITH THESE GIRLS? ... 96
DISCUSSION QUESTIONS ... 96

WHAT IS BEING DONE? ... 97
MEDICAL – RELATED TO VIOLENCE ... 97
MISSIONARIES, MINISTRIES AND NGOs ... 97
GOVERNMENTS ... 98
NIGERIAN MILITARY ... 102
HOW YOU CAN HELP ... 104
DISCUSSION QUESTIONS ... 105

IS IT WORTH IT? ... 107
WHAT DO CHRISTIANS BELIEVE? ... 107
WHY DO CHRISTIANS ALLOW THEMSELVES TO BE KILLED? ... 111
WHY DO CHRISTIANS REFUSE TO DENY CHRIST? ... 120
CONCLUSION ... 124
DISCUSSION QUESTIONS ... 125

IN MEMORY OF ... 127
CHRISTIAN DEATHS BY BOKO HARAM ... 128
CHRISTIAN DEATHS BY FULANI ... 129

WHAT IS TO COME IN 2015? ... 131
FULANI ... 131
BOKO HARAM ... 132
OTHER ... 133

MAPS ... 135

METHODOLOGY ... 139
RESEARCH ... 139
DATABASE ... 139
LIMITATIONS ... 142

ABOUT THE AUTHOR ... 146

CONNECT WITH LAURA	147
ACKNOWLEDGMENTS	**148**
IMAGE, MAP, & PHOTO CREDITS..	**149**
COVER PAGE IMAGE	149
INTRODUCTION..	149
NIGERIA	149
HAUSA-FULANI	150
BOKO HARAM	150
IS IT WORTH IT?	151
IN MEMORY OF	153
MAPS..	153
ENDNOTES	**154**

Introduction

Genocide. What is it? The mere thoughts and images that are evoked by using this word are more than can be put on paper. Yet they must be. The world has been privy to much genocide: genocide by the Nazis, genocide in Rwanda, the Armenian genocide... the list goes on. In fact, the world is watching a genocide take place in Iraq and Syria by the group that calls itself the Islamic State.

Yet as that group wields its might in the Middle East, another genocide is taking place right under our noses. It's happening in Africa. It's happening in Nigeria.

Genocide:[1] *Any of the following acts with the intent to destroy, in whole or in part, a national, ethnical, racial or religious group, as such:*

   a) *Killing members of the group;*
   b) *Causing serious bodily or mental harm to members of the group;*
   c) *Deliberately inflicting on the group conditions of life calculated to bring about its physical destruction in whole or in part;*
   d) *Imposing measures intended to prevent births within the group;*
   e) *Forcibly transferring children of the group to another group.*

Christians are being destroyed by acts of violence, intimidation, rape, kidnapping and murder by the terrorist group Boko Haram and the Fulani tribe. In an effort to oust Christians from Nigeria and establish an Islamic Caliphate, Boko Haram has equaled Islamic State in its violence and controlled territory. The Fulani tribe, originally in dispute with

Christian farmers over cattle grazing land, has turned its attention to eradicating Christianity from Nigeria.

> **Christian Deaths 2014**
>
> By Boko Haram: 3,043 – 4,733
>
> By Fulani: 1,075 - 1,529

This report is intended to examine the persecution in Nigeria against Christians using qualitative (i.e.-stories, news, etc.), as well as quantitative (data and numbers), analysis. Throughout this book, you will understand who the players are, why they do what they do, and what is or isn't being done. You will learn about the plight of these people, how they are responding, and what you can do. Most importantly, you will know their story. You will see that evil exists and, hopefully, you will be motivated to stand up and declare that genocide in Nigeria is not something the world can stand by and allow to happen.

This book is organized so that you can read it cover-to-cover, section-by-section, or out of order completely! It is entirely up to you. Read and re-read the book, move back and forth between sections.

You are the leader in your journey through Nigeria's untold genocide.

Nigeria

History (condensed)

Before becoming independent, Nigeria was a British colony. Britain colonized Nigeria in 1849. During the early 20th century, the future wife of Baron Lugard, a colonial administrator, coined the name. It is derived from the words Niger and Area, referring to the River Niger that runs through Nigeria.[2]

Nigeria derived its independence in 1960 and soon became the Federal Republic of Nigeria with Abuja as its capital. It would eventually be comprised of 36 states and one Federal Capital Territory (FCT). This is very similar to the way the United States is set up: 50 states and DC, each state having its own capital and the FCT being the capital for the entire country.

Although Nigeria became independent in 1960, the current constitution did not come about until 1999, after 16 years of military rule. Although there are irregularities and violence in regards to elections, Nigeria is currently experiencing its longest period of civilian rule. In January 2014, Nigeria assumed a non-permanent seat on the UN Security Council for the 2014-2015 term.[3]

The road to the current Nigeria was fraught with coups, violence, and corruption. Shortly after independence, the military intervened in the country's politics and, with the exception of a 4-year period, the military administered the country. There were military coups in 1966 (twice), 1975, 1976, 1983, 1985, and 1993.[4]

In addition, there was a bloody civil war from 1967 to 1970 that left 2 million Nigerians dead. This led to the change from a British parliamentary style government to an American-style presidential system of separate executive and legislative branches.[5] It should be noted that for criminal proceedings, the Northern States have adopted Sharia Law, leading to tensions between the Muslim and Christian communities.

President	Goodluck Jonathan
Vice President	Mohammed Namadi Sambo
Population 178 million	Christian: 40% Muslim: 50% Other: 10%
Ethnic Groups	Hausa & Fulani: 29% Yoruba: 21% Igbo (Ibo): 18% Ijaw: 10% Kanuri: 4% Ibibio: 3.5 % Tiv: 2.5% There are more than 371 ethnic groups. The above groups are the most populous.
Language	English (official) Hausa Yoruba Igbo Fulani 500 additional indigenous languages
Natural Resources	Natural Gas Petroleum Tin Iron Ore Coal Limestone Lead Zinc Niobium Arable Land
Agriculture Products	Cocoa, peanuts, cotton, palm oil, corn, rice, sorghum, millet, cassava, yams, rubber: cattle, sheep, goats, pigs; timber; fish

Symbols

Flag

The Nigerian flag was designed by Taiwo Akinkunmi in 1958, voted on in 1959, and first hoisted on Nigeria's first day of independence, October 1, 1960. The flag is divided into three equal parts; the outer two sections are green, representing agriculture, and the middle section is white, representing unity and peace.[6]

Coat of Arms[7]

The Nigerian coat of arms has many points of significance. The black shield represents the fertile soil and the two silver bands denote the Niger and Benue rivers. These two rivers form the main inland waterways.

The coctus spectabilis flowers (red) are located at the bottom in the green. This flower grows wildly in Nigeria and is very colorful.

The eagle stands for strength and the chargers (horses) symbolize dignity.

At the bottom of the coat of arms is the Nigerian motto, "Unity and Faith, Peace and Progress."

National Anthem

The national anthem was adopted in 1978 and is a mixture of the most popular entries in the national contest conducted to pick the new anthem. The winners were: John Ilechukwu, Eme

Etim Akpan, B.A. Ogunnaike, Sotu Omoigui, and P.O. Aderibigbe/Benedict Elide Odiase.

WORDS
Arise, O Compatriots,
Nigeria's call and obey,
To serve our fatherland
With love and strength and faith.
The labor of our heroes past
Shall never be in vain
To serve with heart and might
One nation bound in freedom,
Peace and unity.

Oh God of creation,
Direct our noble cause.
Guide our leaders right
Help our youths the truth to know
In love and honesty to grow
And living just and true
Great lofty heights attain
To build a nation where peace
And justice shall reign.

National Pledge
I pledge to Nigeria my country
To be faithful, loyal and honest
To serve Nigeria with all my strength
To defend her unity and uphold her honor and glory
So help me God.

Ethnic, Religious, and Other Identities

There are three ethnic groups that dominate the country: Hausa-Fulani, Igbo, and Yoruba. A person in Nigeria will identify most with their ethnic identity, not Nigeria. There is really not much of a national identity.

"Ethnicity in Nigeria has a significant impact on a person's experiences, perceptions of injustice, social and educational opportunities and much more."[8]

Because of these strong ethnic identities, where a person is born can directly affect their daily life. All official documents require the applicant to identify their place of birth. This one piece of information identifies you as a certain ethnic group. Should a person go out of their local area, they are likely to face discrimination on all levels. This affects where they can work, where they can live, and what services they have access to.

This type of discrimination also happens for religious reasons and non-indigenous reasons. Christians born in the south but migrated to the north have difficulty getting official documents where they live. They generally have to go back to their town of birth. This is also true of Hausa-Fulani children. To obtain birth certificates, the family must travel to a Hausa-Fulani city despite having lived in their current city for generations. Many times, these types of discrimination have a combination of motives. A Christian from the south can migrate to the north. When he has an issue with a person in the North who is most likely Muslim, it is not just a religion-based discrimination. It can also be ethnic as they are definitely of different ethnic origin as well as an indigenous issue (the Christian is not indigenous to the North). Therefore, most of these types of discrimination can be categorized simply as "you are different than me."

Tribe	Christian	Muslim
Hausa-Fulani	5%	95%
Igbo	98%	0%
Yoruba	35%	55%

This ethnic identity situation manifests itself in government as well. The strong ethnic ties lead to cronyism and corruption in the government. Politicians want to help their own people before helping others. They offer wealthy government positions to others in their ethnic group, whether or not the person is qualified, and give financial aid and/or projects to those areas the ethnic group lives in. Should an elected politician not do this, he would face a coup, non-reelection, being ostracized and more. This places ethnic group interests over national interests.

Government, Economy, Military, & Crime

Nigerians have very little trust in their government. A system of ethnic politics, corruption, and cronyism, a widespread lack of services, low quality education, lack of reliable electricity and a whole array of grievances reinforce the distrust of the government.[9] In addition, the military interventions (coups) and the lack of popular support for the policies of the military-run government have laid much distrust at the feet of the military as well. The frequency of coups, coupled with bad governing and a civil war, has set Nigeria back economically, to say the least. These issues have set the stage for violent extremist groups like Boko Haram.

Political Parties
- Accord Party (ACC)
- Action Congress of Nigeria (ACN)
- All Nigeria Peoples Party (ANPP
- All Progressives Congress
- All Progressives Grand Alliance (APGA)
- Congress for Progressive Change (CPC)
- Democratic Peoples Party (DPP)
- Labor Party
- Peoples Democratic Party (PDP)

Government

Nigeria is currently a Federal Republic. It is a mixed legal system of English common law, Islamic law (in the 12 northern states), and traditional law. [10] Nigerians elect their leaders, although their elections are often marred by violence. The election that brought in the current President is viewed as the first legitimate one. Despite being considered legitimate, it was still marred with violence.[11] The next election for President is going to be held in February 2015 and is already teeming with heated debates and accusations from all sides as a former President, who is Muslim and from the North, runs against the current President, who is Christian and from the South. The first two weeks of 2015 have already brought multiple instances of violence.

Its own citizens as well as international governments and organizations perceive the Nigerian government as incredibly corrupt. However, this is the status quo for Nigeria.

> *In Nigeria, the powerful make decisions based on what they believe are required for their political survival and the economic security of their family, clan, and close associates. They have often used illegal and extrajudicial means to coerce or eliminate those who might oppose them.*[12]

In addition, the local governments that receive significant money from the federal government misappropriate their funds. The little that is not misappropriated is often used to benefit just one group. Thus, the political system is looked at, not as a body to serve the people, but as a way to obtain wealth.[13]

Economy

Nigeria has emerged as Africa's largest economy, with 2013 GDP estimated at US$502 billion.[14] Oil is a dominant source of revenue for Nigeria, and has been since the 1970's. Agriculture, telecommunications and services also help to bolster GDP.

Currently, the government is looking to develop stronger public-private partnerships for roads, agriculture and power. This is largely due to significant problems regarding inadequate power supply, lack of infrastructure, and restrictive trade policies that hamper economic growth and investment.

Nigeria faces rampant corruption, a slow and ineffective judicial system, insecurity, lack of proper dispute resolution, and an inefficient property registration system.[15] These issues hamper growth and restrict a decline in extreme poverty levels (over 62% are in extreme poverty).

As already discussed, there are significant disparities in who receives aid/funding from the government. Those that work in the government are significantly wealthier than anyone else in Nigeria and display their wealth for all to see. This kind of disparity finds its way into the judicial system as well. Those with connections and wealth receive better treatment. Nigeria is truly a country of have's and have-nots. Those in government have and those not in government have-not. The disparity adversely affects any chance for economic growth.

> University Professor: $2,500/month
> Local Government Chairman: $7,500+/month
>
> This creates an incentive for doctors, scientists, and academics to leave their professions and go into politics just to make money. Once in office, the person feels societal obligations to better their families and friends. This leads to cronyism and corruption.

Military

At this time, Nigeria's Armed Forces include the Army, Navy and Air Force. Defense spending is less than 1% of Nigeria's GDP. You must be 18 years of age to join and it is completely voluntary. The military is open to both men and women and is estimated to be at about a 50-50 ratio.[16]

There is much dissention and controversy within and about the military in Nigeria. This is mostly due to its conflicts with Boko Haram and the Fulani tribe. There are accusations of the military personnel aiding the attackers. The military has often abandoned its posts and weaponry in face of battles with Boko Haram. The military blames the government for not properly equipping it and for being inconsistent with pay. Morale is considered to be very low and military families have been known to protest against the military's operations against Boko Haram.

Crime & Terrorism

Nigeria is rift with terrorism and crime. The North is riddled with attacks from Boko Haram. The Fulani tribes are consistently in violent conflict with Christian farmers. The South is inundated with political violence over oil. There is drug and human trafficking, smuggling, terrorism, violent crime, piracy, money laundering, and money counterfeiting.
In addition, there is evidence of weapons trafficking, kidnapping, armed robbery and car- jacking.[17] The amount of deaths due to public violence in Nigeria doubled from 2013 to 2014, to over 21,000.[18]

The Global Terrorism Index, an index of all terror-related incidents around the world, placed Nigeria as 4th in the world for terrorist attacks for 2013.[19] However, Boko Haram significantly passed this number mid-2014.

The list of things going wrong in Nigeria is extensive. The military, government, and police have their work cut out for them.

Discussion Questions

1) Do you think that having different criminal law proceedings in the North creates more problems within Nigeria? (North uses Sharia Law while the rest of Nigeria uses secular law)

2) How can Nigerians overcome the ethnic, religious, and indigenous discrimination?

3) How can Nigeria create a Nigerian identity that unites its citizens?

4) Do you think Nigeria can actually have peace and unity? What will it take to achieve it?

Hausa-Fulani

The Hausa and Fulani tribes are actually two separate entities. They have two histories that merged in the 1800s. Although there are still differences between the two tribes, and they maintain their separate identities, many refer to them as one people.

Today, the two tribes are generally referred to as one, Hausa-Fulani. Because of the cultural similarities between the two tribes, and the integration of the two during the 1800's, they have practically merged into one tribe. This proves to be the case even more when referring to politics.[20] The Hausa-Fulani tribe has controlled Nigerian politics for much of Nigerian's independent history.

> There are over 371 tribes in Nigeria. The Hausa-Fulani tribe is the largest and has the most influence.

However, this group of people is referred to as Hausa-Fulani, Hausa, Fulani, and many other names. It is hard to distinguish when it is just one tribe acting, or the two in concert. This is due to the intermingling of the two tribes and their similarities in culture and religion.

For the purposes of this book, "Hausa-Fulani" will be used when referring to the political realm of things. "Fulani" will be used when referencing the disputes between cattle grazers and farmers. This distinction is used because the two tribes create one large political force, yet only the Fulani are typically involved in cattle grazing disputes. The switch to using "Fulani" for cattle grazing disputes is because this topic tends to relate only to Fulani tribesmen, and not the Hausa tribe.

Hausa Tribe

The Hausa tribe in Nigeria is comprised of almost 30 million people: 99.9% are Muslim, the remaining 0.1% are Christian (with .04% being evangelical). Their main language is Hausa, which is rapidly becoming the chief language of Northern Nigeria despite the country's official language being English. The Hausa tribe can also be found in Chad, Ghana, and the Ivory Coast.[21]

The Hausa aristocracy adopted Islam in the 11th century. During the 1500's, Islam was introduced to those not in the aristocracy. Those in the urban areas embraced it right away in order to advance their businesses. The Hausa tribe has been heavily involved in long distance trading for centuries. They exchanged gold from the Middle East for leather, crafts, and food. Villagers were less receptive and oftentimes, villages today are only superficially Muslim. However, both urban and village Hausa culture is steeped in Islam and includes a large amount of prejudice toward Christians.[22]

Marriages within the Hausa tribe are arranged. Women and children have their own hut and the man will have his own. Men will often have multiple wives, leading to this type of living arrangement.

Most of the Hausa live in rural farm villages. Their homes are made of grass or dried mud with thatch roofs. Many are farmers, herdsmen or traders. They generally hold a second job with a factory in order to support their family. Compared to other tribes, they live relatively well, although 30% are unemployed and only 50% can read/write.

Fulani Tribe

History
The history of the Fulani tribe is hard to reconstruct. Historians have difficulty providing an accurate account of their entire history. Nomadic heritage, integration, and dis-

integration with surrounding tribes create uncertain conditions for a well-documented tribal history.[23]

The Fulani people appeared in West Africa during the 10th century. They adopted Islam, which increased their feelings of cultural and religious superiority. The tribe settled in the area and intermingled with other ethnic groups and became known as outstanding clerics.[24]

The movement of the Fulani people into West Africa seems to be peaceful. They were given land grants and their dairy products were highly prized. Over time the number of converts to Islam increased and the Fulani people started resenting being ruled by non-Muslim people. This led to the holy wars in the early 1800s.[25]

In the "holy wars" of 1804 and 1808, the Hausa were conquered by the Fulani tribe (the Fulani were their Islamic neighbors). The Fulani subjugated the Hausa until the early 1900's.

The Fulani people entered into Nigeria a little differently than the rest of West Africa. Nigeria had progressed more than the other West African states. So the Fulani settled in as clerics among the Hausa people. Eventually they would start filling the elite positions within the Hausa populations; such as judges and teachers. Although the Hausa culture influenced these Fulani people (the Fulani even started speaking the Hausa language instead of their own), the Nigerian Fulani people did not lose touch with the rest of the Fulani tribes throughout West Africa and retained their connection with cattle.[26]

In the 1800s, when the Fulani tribes outside of Nigeria revolted against their non-Muslim rulers over what they thought was an unfair cattle tax, the Nigerian Fulani did the same. Some Hausa joined the Fulani after the victory. Others were eased out of positions of power. This time period led to the Fulani instituting themselves as a ruling aristocracy within Nigeria. The Nigerian Fulani then forged alliances with their fellow (non-Nigerian) Fulani, establishing an empire, called the Sokoto Caliphate.[27]

Today

The Fulani people are still very connected with cattle. It is a part of their culture and is considered a part of their identity. Whether they are Urban Fulani or Rural Fulani, they are always tied to each other and to cattle. This leads to the clashes between Fulani and Christians.

The Fulani believe that they can graze their cattle wherever they wish, with impunity. Because the Fulani do not respect Christians and their beliefs, it is not only permissible, but also encouraged to graze cattle on Christian land.

Often, reports documenting these issues name the perpetrators as "cattlemen," "cattle rustlers," "Muslims," and others. This use of local vernacular makes it hard to fully grasp the magnitude of the issue. In addition, attacks by the Fulani are often categorized, by the authorities, as criminal behavior not Fulani-instigated. Therefore, the number of attacks is likely to be higher than what is in this study. However, it is very clear that the Fulani want the Christians gone for religious and land purposes.

> *Most mainstream media mentioned vague accusations of cattle theft or unsupported statements of political and land disputes as possible motivations for the attacks. However, in recent months Muslim Fulani herdsmen have increased the unprovoked slaughter of unarmed Christians in their homes that has taken place for several years in Plateau state.*[28]

Hausa-Fulani Politics

There is no question that the Hausa-Fulani create a very effective political machine. As mentioned before, they have controlled most of politics since the inception of Nigeria. This ended in 2011 when Goodluck Jonathan, a Christian, was elected leader. Many attribute the current instability in Nigeria to this point in time.

When Nigeria gained its independence, Islamic courts were limited to family law only. Criminal law moved to a secular court system. This, along with other similar happenings, led to political and spiritual movements within the Islamic society in Nigeria, allowing for extremist views to be perpetuated. These extremist views were not just in relation to terrorism, but also to politics.[29]

The Hausa-Fulani maintain their determination that they should be the ruling power in Nigeria.

> *"The new nation called Nigeria should be an estate of our great grandfather Othman Dan Fodio. We must ruthlessly prevent a change of power. We use the minorities in the north as willing tools and the south as a conquered territory and never allow them to rule over us and never allow them to have control over their future."*[30]

In 2010, General Buhari (a Muslim) was running against Goodluck Jonathan (a Christian). Although politics can always be brutal emotionally, General Buhari sent it to a new level.

> *"Lynch Christians in the North if [we] lose the 2011 Presidential election."*[31]

But it wasn't just the General that felt this way.

> *"Northerners would make Nigeria ungovernable for President Goodluck if he wins the Presidential ticket and that the North should not be responsible for any disaster that will face the country if Jonathan emerged as president in 2011."*[32]

Needless to say, General Buhari lost the election. Goodluck Jonathan became President. There has been no peace ever since. The Hausa-Fulani give passive, if not active, support to Boko Haram and to the attacks by Fulanis on Christians.

In late 2013, groups of indigenous people in Nigeria came together to protest any political candidate (for 2015) that had links with Boko Haram. They said the conflict had led to the displacement of indigenous communities and the seizure of ancestral homelands, as well as rape and killings of innocent civilians. The groups noted that a statement by spokesman of the Northern Elders Forum, Prof. Ango Abdullahi, that the Hausa-Fulani will "never return power to the South" once the region obtained it, demonstrated a malicious show of arrogance that must be resisted by Nigerians.[33]

> *"We condemn in strong terms the current realignment of political forces, which has not taken into consideration the interests of indigenous peoples but has been tailored only to promote the wishes and aspirations of the northern caliphate against the genuine interest of the indigenous communities. It said Hausa-Fulani political groups are interested in nothing but a system that will sustain and oil their own parochial and self-serving interests saying that little wonder that the violent Boko Haram has become a political scare crow for a section of the Hausa-Fulani political class. The responses of the northern caliphate to the series of bombings have been that of cold complicity."*[34]

Whether or not the Hausa-Fulani actively support Boko Haram is a question that cannot yet be answered. It is known that there are Hausa-Fulani sections within Boko Haram.[35] There are Hausa-Fulani people that actively participate in Boko Haram activities. However, there has not been a definitive link between the Hausa-Fulani nation as a whole and Boko Haram. They may both want to eradicate Christians. They may both hate the Nigerian government as it stands today. They both want an Islamic Caliphate. But right now, there does not yet appear to be an overt, direct connection.

Fulani and Christians

The Fulani are vehemently prejudiced against Christians. In addition to opposing Christianity's existence in the area, the Fulani fully believe that all land is available for their cattle. Therefore, the Fulani can graze their cattle wherever they please. In the eyes of the Fulani, it matters not that Christians legally own the land for farming.

Caused by Fulani	2014
Christians Displaced	180,000+
Christians Killed	1,057+
Houses Burned	581+
Churches Burned	19+

These conflicts have been going on for many years. Recently, however, the Fulani have become increasingly violent in their attacks and the frequency of attacks has increased significantly.

Between May and November (6 months) of 2013, Benue state's Agatu Local Government Area saw deadly attacks on Christian farmers, by the Fulani, that displaced an estimated 10,000 people. In addition, at least 205 were killed. The news media reports no motive. Christian leaders, however, say the motive is to remove Christians from the area by demoralizing and eventually destroying them.

Christian leader from Agatu, John Ngbede, confirmed the attacks:

> *"It is true that Agatu is under attack by Muslim Fulani herdsmen at the moment. Many of our Christian brethren have been killed. The Muslim gunmen that are attacking our Christian communities are numerous; they are so many that we can't count them. They are spread across all the communities and unleashing terror on our people without any security resistance."[36]*

The Fulani want Christians gone. They believe the land belongs to them and their cattle. Laws and rules of ownership mean nothing to them and they will do whatever is necessary to achieve this. Their escalating brutality is evidence of this.

In Fadan Karshi, the Rev. Kefas Sai Wujun, archdean of the Gimi Conference of the ERCC, told Morning Star News that his neighbor, the wife of a retired pastor, was among 13 Christians killed in the September 17 attack on that town – the third armed assault on Fadan Karshi since May.

> *"To be sincere and candid, I find no justifiable reason for the Fulanis to keep attacking this town. We've heard that the Fulanis have vowed to destroy this town completely. They vowed that they will continue to attack the town until it is deserted and become a grazing land for them. I don't know how they intend to achieve this, but the frequent attacks are pointers to the desire to achieve this aim."[37]*

It isn't just about the land anymore. The Fulani are massacring innocent people. They are burning down churches and disrupting worship services. It is no longer a dispute between a few people when some trespass onto the land and destroy the crops of others. These types of attacks go beyond disputes over land. They are about wiping out Christianity and its adherents.

> *"These attacks on Christian members of our churches have disrupted church activities, as Christians can no longer worship together in their congregations,"* Rev. David Bello.[38]

> *"Life has become unbearable for our church members who have survived these attacks, and they are making worship services impossible,"* Rev. Michael Apochi.[39]

> *"They were saying, 'We have killed and destroyed these infidels, and we must take possession of their lands; here we shall establish an Islamic state,' and this is evidence that we are facing a genocide against Christians in this state and in northern Nigeria,"* the Rt. Rev. Timothy Yahaya.[40]

In addition to disrupting services, the Fulani have all but told the Christian community that the Fulani intend to wipe them out.

> *"The Fulani gunmen yesterday [Jan 8, 2014], dropped a letter in the town warning Christians to be prepared for a total war in the coming weeks,"* Solomon Musa.[41]

And the war came…

Direct-victim-link reporting puts Christian deaths, by the Fulani at 1,075 for 2014. What does this figure mean? Direct reporting is when the news article, government report, etc. specifically states that Fulani people killed Christians. In some capacity, the accounting of the incident leads to the understanding that the crime was committed by the Fulani against Christians. It should be noted that if the report uses phrases that are known to represent the Fulani, they are counted as Fulani.[42]

There are 454 deaths where the victims were not clearly identified in any capacity.

As we look at these numbers, we see between 1,075 and 1,529 Christian deaths at the hands of the Fulani. But is this the whole story? Unfortunately, it is not. Christian leaders in Taraba state put out a statement, in August, that 76 Christians had been killed since March. So, from March through July, 76 people had died in Taraba state alone. However, media reporting puts it at 58. Another example is in Kaduna, where leaders put the death toll to over 600 (January-August) but the media reporting only accounts for 482. It is apparent that many incidents are either not reported, or the death tolls are never updated and re-published. These types of errors in reporting are frequent and lend credence to the assumption that the number of deaths of Christians is actually much higher than is reported.

> *Every time we eat meat we should wonder how many Nigerian boys, girls and babies are dead, displaced, deprived just because we eat meat. In Nigeria cow meat is murderous business.*

Another thing to keep in mind, Nigeria has 36 states and 1 Federal Capitol Territory. Taraba was reporting for one state over a five-month period. That five-month period saw 58 Christians dying in Taraba by the Fulani (not counting those deaths that were undetermined). That same reporting had 336 deaths across Nigeria by the Fulani against Christians (again, does not include those that are undetermined).

In addition to killing many Christians, reporting indicates 182,000 Christians displaced due to Fulani attacks. This number is likely low. It is not common to report the number of displaced persons. In addition, when whole villages are wiped out, there is no one to report on those that ran away.

What is the take away?

1) Death toll statistics reported through media are not wholly reliable. There are many deaths that go unreported. The numbers reported in the media are generally less than the actual amount.

2) There are many instances where numbers are not included. Instead words such as "many," "several," and "scores" are used. Although these give a general context, they do not aid in determining a numerical value.

3) Many times the reports do not specifically say that the Fulani were the culprits or that Christians were the victims. Additionally, there remain many reports that just do not say one way or the other. Reports that definitively identify the culprits and victims are not incorporated in the numbers in this report.

These three points show that the number of Christians that have died and/or been injured by the hands of the Fulani tribe are likely higher than is reported.

News Stories & Witness Accounts

This section is by no means exhaustive. However, in order to fully appreciate what is going on in any situation, accounts by people who have lived it are necessary. In this section you will find a few cases that have been covered by worldwide media, as well as witness accounts. These serve to show the side of things that facts and data cannot. It is an insight into the constant struggle and the continual obstacles that many face in Nigeria.

These stories are reports by news agencies, Non Government Organizations (NGOs) and religious organizations. Some are condensed down or reconstructed, but most are the full story, exactly as reported.

Because the stories are so numerous, they cannot all be accounted for in this book. In addition, the overall meaning is often lost if too much time is spent in the horrific details. It only takes one example of a beheading to understand the horrific nature of the action. Therefore, no more than one account is needed.

Hopefully, these chosen stories will help you get into the minds, the feelings, and the lives of Christians in Nigeria.

Cattlemen[43]
"The cattlemen who attacked my village were more than 40 – they were armed with guns and other weapons. As I talk to you, there is no single house that has not been destroyed as the attackers set fire on our houses. As we made efforts to escape from being killed, our attackers shot at every one they saw. It was a miracle that I escaped alive."

Fulani Slaughter[44]
"They are burning down houses and killing our Jukun Christian brothers. They slaughtered children and women like rams. As I am talking to you right now, over twenty people have been killed, with several others sustaining various degrees of injuries while several houses have been burnt."

Shonong Massacre[45]
Survivors of Monday's (Jan. 6) slaughter of 33 Christians in a village in Nigeria's Plateau state said Special Task Force (STF) soldiers stationed to protect them turned their weapons on those fleeing the attack.

Speaking from her hospital bed with bullet wounds in her legs, 25-year-old Antele Alamba told Morning Star News that hundreds of Muslim Fulani herdsmen armed with guns and machetes attacked Shonong village in Riyom Local Government

Area without provocation, burning homes and butchering women and children.

"The soldiers stationed in the village to protect us joined the Fulani herdsmen in shooting, and in the process most of our people were killed," Alamba said as tears dripped down her cheeks. "I was shot by soldiers I ran to for protection. We were all trapped in the village as there was no way of escape for us. We ran to the premises of the church, and some soldiers followed us there. They were shooting and the herdsmen were shooting too. It was chaos and confusion everywhere."

Pastors of the Church of Christ in Nations (COCIN) conducted a funeral service on Tuesday (Jan. 7) for the 33 slain Christians amid tight security provided by soldiers, sources said.

Asing Alamba, 70, sustained bullet and machete wounds in the Shonong attack.

Alamba, receiving treatment at Vom Christian Hospital near Jos, said the herdsmen killed the first Christian on Sunday (Jan. 5). The next morning, word reached the village that Fulani herdsmen accompanied by a soldier had attacked a local Christian, Andrew Bature, his wife and others when he went to his farm.

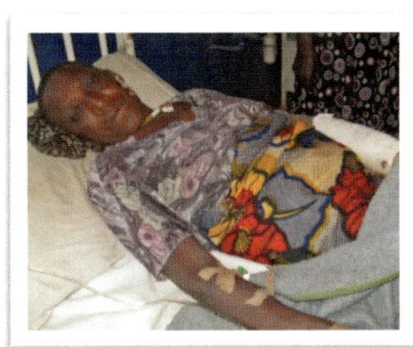

"He and the women were attacked, and he was killed by Muslim Fulani herdsmen," Alamba said. "His wife and the women who ran back to the village said Andrew Bature was killed by a band of Muslim herdsmen led by one of the soldiers stationed in our village by the name Aminu."

Villagers went to the farm and brought back Bature's body, she said.

"In less than 15 minutes of their return with the remains of Andrew Bature, hundreds of Fulani herdsmen armed with guns surrounded our village and began shooting everyone they saw," said Alamba. "They set fire on houses and either shot or butchered our women, children and the elderly."

Alamba, a student of environmental health at the School of Health Technology, Zawan, near Jos, said she miraculously escaped and trekked to neighboring Fang village, where Christians took her to the hospital. Residents of Fang had come to Shonong to help repel the attackers.

Alamba said the soldiers who had been shooting into the air and shouting on Sunday night (Jan. 5) had demanded that area resident Jidauna Mwangwong open his shop to provide them alcoholic drinks, but that he had refused because of the late hour. They forced another resident to open his shop, but not before insulting Mwangwong and telling them that "they would see how he will open his shop" the following morning, she said.

"After the soldiers drank themselves out, they went back to their duty posts and continued with the shooting into the air," Alamba said.

Another survivor, 22-year-old Edward Iliya, said the raid was a collaborative effort by the soldiers and herdsmen.

"Twenty of us went to the farm of Andrew Bature to retrieve his corpse minutes before the attack occurred, and I was almost shot by one of the soldiers because he pointed his gun at me to shoot me when I dived for cover and scampered away," Iliya told Morning Star News. "I was in the village at the time of the attack. We were trapped in the village with no hope of escaping as the rampaging herdsmen attacked us in all directions. God in his infinite mercies caused Christians from our neighboring village of Fang to rush here to assist us. They repelled the Fulani gunmen, and we found ways to escape from the attackers."

Iliya, a student at Federal College of Land Resources Technology, Kuru, near Jos, said 22-year-old David Gwong, son of the Shonong COCIN pastor, was among those killed in the attack. The pastor has fled the village, he said.

"Right now the entire village has been destroyed, and there are no more houses to return to," said Iliya, uninjured but assisting victims at the hospital. "When we there yesterday for the burial of our dead relatives, there were only three houses left that were not burned by the attackers."

The Rev. Yakubu Fom, pastor of the COCIN congregation at Riyom town, told Morning Star News that the victims' corpses were recovered amid charred houses and surrounding bushes.

Fom lamented that soldiers and other members of security agencies stationed in Shonong village did not keep Muslim attackers from murdering elderly Christian women and children in their homes.

"One wonders what the soldiers were doing in the village while the Muslim Fulani herdsmen killed and set fire on homes of our members without the soldiers repelling them," Fom said.

"They were all murdered by the Muslim Fulani herdsmen," she said.

All of those killed, she said, were members of the Shonong COCIN congregation.

The church has about 300 members. Shonong also has a local congregation of Evangelical Church Winning All.

Soka Forest of Horror[46]

"The herdsmen lived there and made a camp just outside the building where the captives were chained and abused. They grazed their cattle over the decomposing bodies every day and they shared the same environment with the alleged kidnappers."

"Why did they feel comfortable with the sight of these bodies and why is the police quiet about this possible link to all the activities and murder at the site?" asked Mr. Olabimtan Isaiah, one of the residents.

"We saw more of the herdsmen in the area and especially along the Ogunpa River bank where they rear their cattle. Most of the bodies and the building were found along that river," added Isaiah.

Fulani and Boko Haram

Fulani attack mostly Christian communities. Boko Haram attacks mostly Christian communities. Both groups take a hard line approach to Islam. Because of these consistencies, there are fears that the two groups may be cooperating in an effort to reach the same end-state: no more Christians. The Fulani will get their fields for grazing and Boko Haram will get its caliphate. But are they really working in concert? Or is it just happenstance that they have the same goal in mind: eradicating Christians?

The connections between the Fulani people and Boko Haram are confusing to say the least. Some claim that the Fulani are helping Boko Haram by trafficking weapons and money. Others say that Boko Haram is using the local conflicts of the Fulani as cover for their operations. Others say that they are mutually benefitting from each other.

There are connections between the Fulani and Boko Haram. No one is in doubt as to this fact. Fulani men, once arrested, confessed that they took part in Boko Haram attacks. There have also been instances where Boko Haram members were arrested while disguising themselves as herdsmen. The Fulani have also been caught with assorted arms and ammunition that were on their way to Boko Haram.[47] So it is very evident that there are crossovers between the two groups.

But are they working in concert with each other? The leaders of the respective groups have not pledged allegiance or cooperation with each other. There have been instances of Boko Haram attacking and/or abducting the Fulani people.

> *At least 20 women and girls were reported missing on Thursday at a nomadic settlement, Garkin Fulani, near Chibok town, Borno State, after gunmen suspected to be members of the Boko Haram staged a midday abduction.* [48]

Whether or not the abduction was intentional has yet to be seen. There are even reports from the military that these reports are untrue and the abductions did not occur.[49] This back and forth makes the determination of potential collaboration very difficult.

Based on reporting, it appears that there are Fulani people who sympathize with Boko Haram and join in Boko Haram's activities. It also appears that the Fulani take note of what Boko Haram is doing and imitate their tactics. Many Christian leaders believe that Islamic extremist groups, like Boko Haram, are inciting the Fulani. They fear that the Fulani, with the backing from these groups, want to take over the Christian areas in order acquire land for grazing, stockpile arms and expand Islamic territory.[50]

> *"The farmers [Christians] and herdsmen [Fulani] have always fought. Why is it that only now they are using highly sophisticated weapons? Come on. They're getting sophisticated weapons and support from somewhere. They are attacking police, police stations, military barracks, government buildings,*

> *and innocent people. Clearly somebody else is supporting them."*[51]

Some Christian leaders go even further, espousing that Boko Haram comes in and joins the Fulani in their attacks. In Taraba state, Muslims in military uniforms are fighting alongside ethnic Fulani men. In one instance, they stormed two churches and killed 31 people as they worshipped.

> *"The attack on Christians in Taraba state is a planned genocide against Christians by Islamic insurgents who have invaded the southern part of the state, inhabited mostly by Christians, since February,"* Rev. Caleb Ahema.[52]

In addition, Fulani men are joining the ranks of Boko Haram and bringing their new knowledge of warfare to the rest of the Fulani people. The Fulani have adapted to a hit-and-run, guerilla style attack method. They shoot children and hack adults - in their sleep -and burn houses to the ground.[53] These type of tactics make many believe that their motives go beyond land disputes between farmers and cattle grazers. The motives have changed to a desire to eradicate Christians.

> *"It's something you cannot hide. The people that carry out the attacks are terrorists and Fulani by tribe. The decent Fulani we know won't kill people without pity. … There was a time some of us did not belief that the killings in Southern Kaduna have any religious connotation, but from the chanting, it has taking a religious dimension. The government must step up security in the Southern part of Kaduna state"* Rev. Sunday Ibrahim.[54]

Although the property disputes have been longstanding, church leaders say attacks on Christian communities by the Fulani constitute a war "by Islam to eliminate Christianity" in Nigeria.[55] It is apparent that at a minimum, the Fulani are being emboldened by the atrocities being committed by Boko

Haram. At its worst, the Fulani are receiving direct aid from Boko Haram for the Fulani's raids. Whether the relationship between the two is passive or active, it is apparent that the Fulani's intentions have shifted to destroying Christianity within Nigeria and appropriating Christian lands for themselves.

Fulani & Genocide

Although it is unclear whether or not the Fulani are in cooperation with Boko Haram, it is clearly evident that Boko Haram is emboldening the Fulani people. What has always been an issue of land disputes has turned into a deliberate and systematic attempt to exterminate Christians (at a minimum the Christian farmers, if not more) within Nigeria.

For genocide to be declared, one of five conditions has to be met. The Fulani have to have the intent to destroy, in whole or part, Christians.

Killing members of the group

It has been evidenced through this book that the Fulani are killing Christians. In fact, they have murdered a **minimum** of 1,057 Christians in 2014. Christians, specifically, are their target because of their religion and because the Fulani want their land.

Despite their motive, it is still genocide. The word "intent" is separate from "motive." So whether it's religious based, land based or any other motive, the *intent* to kill Christians is, in itself, genocide.

> *"This is the third time that the Muslims have attacked Christians on a Sunday,"* Ahema said. *"The attack led to the death of four persons in Gindin Waya, and 27 persons in Sondi. Among the dead is the pastor of the Sondi church, Nuhu Useni, and his only male child."*[56]

> *"Suddenly we heard sounds of gunshots around our village,"* Awe said. *"The pastor was still in the pastorate when the Muslim Fulani gunmen forced their way onto the church premises. They cut him, his wife, and a daughter with a machete, and then tied the hands and feet of the three of them before setting the house on fire. The three of them were burned to ashes in the living room of the pastorate. We only found the charred remains of the three of them the following morning."*[57]

> *"The gunmen then came onto the church premises and began shooting,"* Wujun said. *"I heard them shouting at the top of their voices, saying they must obliterate any trace of Christianity in the town."*[58]

Through their actions, and through reports of what they say when attacking, it is evident that the Fulani's intentions are to wipe out Christians.

Causing serious bodily or mental harm to members of the group

The Fulani people enact serious bodily and mental harm to Christians. In addition to killing Christians, the survivors are often burned, butchered, and maimed. Their mental scars are even worse. Many have lost their whole family, their house, their livelihood, and more. Those that survive are consumed with fear.

> *"Five of the members of my church were killed while they were on their farms,"* Wujun said. *"The situation is so bad that people no longer go to their farms because of fear of the unknown, and also children no longer go to school. Surviving parents have transferred their children who are pupils out to other towns they think are safer."*[59]

Deliberately inflicting on the group conditions of life calculated to bring about its physical destruction in whole or in part

The conditions that are created by the incessant attacks on Christians by the Fulani people are bringing about an unbearable life for the Christians. Their living conditions have deteriorated; some have no house, others no furniture, many are displaced and living with strangers or in the bush.

> *"There have been as many as 51 separate, targeted attacks in many communities in southern Kaduna, including recent attacks on Takad and Moro'a communities. As a result of these attacks, not less than 600 persons, including old men, old women, young children and babies, are confirmed to have been murdered. Also, not less than 1,060 houses have been burned. Of necessity, tens of thousands of our people are now refugees in their own fathers' land."*[60]

> *"The crisis has forced us into seeing the bitter side of life – we no longer have beds to sleep on,"* Oyigadu said. *"Some of us manage with the mats donated to us by some Christian brethren, and others whose houses were also burned down are still squatting with their relatives in Otukpo town or cities outside Benue state."*[61]

When the Fulani's attacks are changing the quality of life for Christians, are displacing Christians, are depleting churches of their members, and - in essence- disallowing for Christian living, it is genocide.

Imposing measures intended to prevent births within the group

There does not seem to be any measures, at this time, that are specifically intended to prevent Christians from procreating. All measures, at this point in time, seem to be to kill and displace Christians.

Forcibly transferring children of the group to another group
Although many children are being transferred to other areas of the country for their safety, it is not apparent that this is the targeted outcome of the attacks by the Fulani. The Fulani are trying to exterminate Christians, not transfer them.

Conclusion
The Fulani people are guilty of three of the five acts that constitute genocide. International law only requires that one be fulfilled in order to be labeled genocide. The Fulani are killing Christians. They are causing serious physical and mental harm to Christians through their heinous acts. The attacks by the Fulani, on Christians, are enacted in an effort to eradicate Christian existence by using violence, intimidation, and forced displacement. The Fulani are one part of the overall genocide of Christians in Nigeria. With the increased boldness, their part may take on even greater impact in the coming year.

Questions

1) How should the Christians react to the attacks by the Fulani? Should they fight back?

2) Do you think the government is doing all it can to help the Christians? If not, what could they do better?

3) Do you think the Fulani and Boko Haram are acting together? Why or why not?

4) Do you think the Hausa-Fulani people are passive or active in their support of Boko Haram?

5) Do you believe that the Fulani people are providing assistance for Boko Haram by moving weapons and money? Or do you think that it is just a few Fulani people that happen to also support Boko Haram? Why or why not?

Boko Haram

Boko Haram killed at least 1,587 people in 2013 and claimed responsibility for over 90% of all terrorist attacks in Nigeria. They are one of the most deadly terrorist groups in the world with an average of 8 deaths per attack.[62] That was 2013. The following year brought more destruction, more violence, and more death.

Boko Haram came on to the international public scene with the abduction of over 200 girls from a school in Chibok, Borno State, Nigeria. The world's focus moved on, however, with the rise of Islamic State in Syria and Iraq. Despite the world turning away from the issue, Boko Haram continued to wage its war to establish their Islamic Caliphate and has equaled Islamic State's violence[63] and territory grab[64] in Iraq.

History

Boko Haram got its start in 2002 in Maiduguri, Nigeria. Although most know it as Boko Haram, the group's name is actually *Jama'atu Ahlis Sunnar Lidda'awati Walk-Jihad.* This loosely translates to "people committed to the propagation of the Prophet's teachings and jihad."[65] The term "Boko Haram" (meaning "western education is sin") is actually a nickname given by locals because of the group's rejection of Western education.

Mohammad Yusuf founded the group with the aim to establish an Islamic state in Nigeria. This state would incorporate Sharia courts. Although Yusuf was a trained Salafist, the group does not strictly adhere to Salafi doctrine. This is largely due to the group being decentralized and most of the members being poor and uneducated.

Originally, the group was non-violent and focused on withdrawing itself from Nigeria. It felt that Nigeria was too secular and the North, although following Islamic Sharia law, was not enforcing Sharia Law effectively. This doctrine put the group in confrontations with security forces and locals. As time passed, the confrontations became increasingly violent but it wasn't until 2009 that the group radicalized and became the violent group we know today.

> **Salafi:** an ultra-conservative view of Sunni Islam. Adherents consider Sufis to be misguided and outside the fold of Islam. They advocate for the return of social structures from the earliest days of Islam and adhere strictly to Sharia law.

> **Sharia Law:** religious laws based on the Quran. There are varying levels of interpretation. Most Muslim countries have Sharia law in some form. For a Salafi, the earliest Quranic examples should be emulated. For the five *hadd* crimes (unlawful sex, false accusation of unlawful sex, wine drinking, theft, and highway robbery) a person can receive flogging, stoning, amputation, exile or execution. Extremist groups apply the harshest punishments and also exact vigilante justice.

In July 2009, members of Boko Haram refused to follow a motorbike helmet law. While it sounds trivial, the disagreement would later turn violent. Police used heavy-handed tactics to enforce the law, which led to an armed uprising in the northern states of Nigeria. The army stepped in and suppressed the uprising. By the end of it, over 800 people were dead and Yusuf was charged with crimes of terrorism. Following his televised execution, which many believe to be extrajudicial, Boko Haram became radicalized, using suicide bombings, prison breaks, and assassinations to bring about its Islamic state.[66] Although his execution was the catalyst for the group becoming radical and violent, the members were already festering with grievances. The police brutality and impunity, the economic situation of many of the members, and the sectarian conflicts with Christians made the group ripe for violence.[67] Yusuf's execution was the tipping point.

Since the incident in 2009, the group has gone underground and Abubakar Shekau stepped in to fill Yusuf's shoes. Under his leadership, the group has turned extremely violent, leading to its designation as a terrorist group by the United States, Australia, Canada, the United Nations, and the European Union. The group targets Christians, Muslims who are too westernized or don't agree with Boko Haram, schools, and security forces. In addition to targeting institutions related to education or government, the group also focuses on prison breaks.

Boko Haram is decentralized in its structure and organization. This means that although there is leadership at the top, there are many local cells. This allows for the local cell members to carry out attacks at the most opportune moment to inflict the most damage.[68] It also gives Boko Haram the flexibility to act out revenge attacks on villages that oppose the group. These revenge attacks work to discourage villages and towns from resisting a Boko Haram take over.

Boko Haram has also splintered into separate groups. The most well-known of these splinter groups is Ansaru. There are grievances between the two groups over Boko Haram's treatment of Muslims. Some analysts believe that this is the reason for Ansaru operating outside of Nigeria as an "external operations unit."[69]

As a terrorist group, much of Boko Haram's power is based in fear. The more fear it can instill in the populace, the more it can control. Fear leads to chaos. Chaos gives Boko Haram the edge it needs to fulfill its desires. A woman speaking to Christianity Today about the violence against Christians in the North moving to the South said it best:

"That's exactly what Boko Haram wants – to see that everybody is scared and victimized so they can make Nigeria ungovernable and take over."

Leadership

Mohammad Yusuf
AKA: Ustaz Mohammed Yusuf
Born: January 29, 1970 – Girgir Village, Yobe state, Nigeria
Died: July 30, 2009
Family: 4 wives, 12 children

Yusuf is believed to have received instruction in Salafism, and was a strong adherent to the Salafi doctrine. He started the group now known as Boko Haram in an effort to counter the Nigerian government. He felt that good Muslims needed to withdraw from the westernized Nigeria. In its efforts to withdraw itself, the group entered into conflicts with security forces and locals. These conflicts led Yusuf to be on the run in 2004 (fleeing to Saudi Arabia),[70] and eventually to his death in 2009. His death was the catalyst for the group becoming radically violent.

His death is considered by most to be extrajudicial. There are conflicting reports to his capture, his detention and his death. The police attested that he was killed in a shootout while trying to escape the battle. The army said they captured him in battle and handed him over to the police. Reporters were shown two videos: one of Yusuf confessing to police in custody and another that was shown on television showing the police dancing around Yusuf's bullet-ridden body and discussing what may have happened if the case had gone to court.[71]

The incidents, and confusions, around Yusuf's death not only led to the change in tactics by Boko Haram, it also left the general populace with a distrust for their government.

Abubakar Shekau
AKA: Darul Tawheed, Abu Bakr Skilwa, Imam Abu Bakr Shiku, Abu Muhammad Abu Bakr Bin Muhammad Al Shakwi Al Muslimi Bishku
Born: Shekau village in Yobe state, Nigeria
Age: 30's to mid-40's, birth dates used are 1965, 1969, and 1975
Education: Borno State College of Legal and Islamic Studies
Reward: US - $7 million, Nigeria – 50 million Naira
Fluent Languages: Kanuri, Hausa, Arabic, Fulani

As a child, Shekau was sent to Quranic school. He spent 11 years there and was eventually asked to leave because of his continual arguing with the leadership at the school. He had militant and aggressive tendencies from a young age. He then became a street-side mechanic and sold perfume bottles. During this time he preached in the streets, criticizing the Nigerian government for neglecting the northern states of Nigeria.[72]

It was during this time the Shekau came to know Mamman Nur, the man who introduced him to Yusef. The three were very close and when Yusuf was killed, Shekau moved in to assume leadership.

In July 2010, Abubakar Shekau officially announced his leadership of Boko Haram and threatened to attack Western influences in Nigeria. He also made certain to issue a warning that any person opposing him would be killed. He soon expressed solidarity with Al Qaeda and threatened the United States.

Known for his ruthlessness, Shekau ushered in an intensely violent Boko Haram. Boko Haram's operational capabilities have grown extensively under his command. He not only deems this violence as necessary, he relishes it. In 2012, he stated,

> *"I enjoy killing anyone that God commands me to kill – the way I enjoy killing chickens and rams."*

In addition to the violence, Shekau has also expanded the influence of Boko Haram. Instead of focusing on Nigeria, he has declared that Boko Haram will become an international influence.

> *"Let me make it crystal clear to you save you from unnecessary distorted newspapers and the radio analysis on issues you don't understand. We are not fighting the north, we are fighting the world. And you will see us fighting the world. This is our job."*[73]

Shekau does not directly communicate with the media or with his soldiers. He wields his power through a few cell leaders. He heads a 30-person Shura council, which controls the cells in northeast Nigeria. This set up allows Shekau to authorize all decisions and mold Boko Haram to his own vision. It also allows him to be the only one to claim credit for attacks. [74]

Shekau has reportedly been killed three times. The latest claim came in September 2014, but Shekau has been seen in videos since this date. It is unclear if the videos were pre-recorded. The Nigerian government espouses that Shekau is dead and any videos coming out are people impersonating Shekau. To them, Shekau is like the "Dread Pirate Roberts," an entity that is passed down from person to person, creating a never-ending phenomenon. However, the United States is still offering a reward for information leading to his capture and as history has dictated, the Nigerian government's claims are not always factual.

Abu Zaid and Abu Qaqa

These two names are pseudonyms for two men who act as spokespersons to journalists. Their identities are unknown. They communicate with journalists through phone interviews and statements.[75]

Mamman Nur
Citizenship: Cameroon
Connections: AQIM, al Shabaab, AQAP, IMU

Reportedly introduced Shekau and Yusuf. He is also believed to have masterminded the August 2011 bombing of the UN office complex in Abuja (capital of Nigeria).[76] He has significant contacts to international terrorist organizations and runs the international theater for Boko Haram. This includes Pakistan and the Sahel, in addition to Nigeria. Nur is the connection between Boko Haram and the international terrorist players.[77]

Khalid al-Barnawi
It is believed that al-Barnawi left Boko Haram to lead Ansaru, a splinter group. The split is widely assumed to be because of al Qaeda in the Islamic Maghreb (AQIM). Shekau was attacking Nigerians only. Al-Barnawi, and AQIM, believed that Boko Haram should also move outside of Nigeria. Despite the split, the two groups are now working together and it is believed that al-Barnawi is on Boko Haram's Shura council.[78]

Connections, Aid, & Financing

Connections
Al Qaeda Core (AQC) – In 2000 and 2002, Osama bin Laden issued two messages calling on Nigerian Muslims to wage jihad. While bin Laden was in Sudan in the 1990's, he met Mohammed Ali, a Nigerian. It is alleged that bin Laden instructed Ali to organize an extremist cell in Nigeria and was given roughly US$3 million to do so. Ali returned to Nigeria in 2002 and funded extremist groups. Boko Haram was a major beneficiary.[79]

Abu-Mahjin, from Chad, acted as an intermediary between the two groups. In 2009, he contacted AQC for funds to facilitate attacks in Nigeria. Boko Haram started its terror campaign two months after the link was reported.[80]

In August 2011, Boko Haram leaders met with senior al Qaeda leaders in Saudi Arabia during the pilgrimage to Mecca, with the intent to finalize both financial and logistical arrangements with AQC. Following the meeting, a Boko Haram spokesperson, Abu Qaqa, boasted of the new intimate relationship: "We enjoy financial and technical support from them [AQC]. Anything we want from them we ask them." In 2012, a Nigerian intelligence report claimed that Boko Haram received a financial donation from an unidentified group in Algeria. According to the report, Boko Haram received a lump-sum cash support of N40 million (US$265,000) from an Algerian terrorist group. However, Boko Haram has since acquired many more outlets for soliciting cash.[81]

Al Qaeda in the Islamic Maghreb (AQIM) – It is believed that Boko Haram receives limited funding. Boko Haram members have also received training at AQIM training camps.[82] When Yusuf was killed, AQIM's leader offered his "Salafist brothers" in Nigeria "men, weapons, and ammunition to gain revenge on Nigeria's ruling Christian minority. At least 800 Yusuf followers fled Nigeria to answer AQIM's call for help.[83]

In 2014, AQIM released a statement offering training, supplies and militants to the Boko Haram cause. The group has also provided financing through donation organizations in Great Britain and Saudi Arabia. It also supplied weapons. The groups conduct joint operations in Mali.[84]

Al Shabaab – It is believed by the US government that these two organizations share money and explosive materials.[85] Mamman Nur is also reported to have received trainings from al Shabaab in Somalia before he launched the attack against the United Nations Headquarters in Abuja, Nigeria.[86]

Ansar al-Dine – The two organizations fight alongside each other in Mali.[87]

Ansaru – A splinter group of Boko Haram and collaborates with the group. It is believed that Ansaru's leader is also a ranking member of Boko Haram's Shura council. In addition, it is believed that some of the kidnappings (mostly the kidnapping of foreigners) are done by Ansaru and then transferred to Boko Haram.[88]

Fulani Tribes – members of the Fulani tribe have admitted to also being members of Boko Haram. In addition, they bring Boko Haram tactics back to their tribesmen and emulate the terrorist group. It is thought that the Fulani tribes may be moving weapons and cash for Boko Haram. It is unclear whether these are the local Nigerian Fulani tribes or tribes outside of Nigeria.

Movement for the Unity of Jihad in West Africa (MUJAO) – Operational support.[89]

Nigerian Government – Boko Haram has allies within the government that funnel weapons, intelligence, money, and information to the group.[90] In addition, the group often acts with impunity due to its connections within the government. Actors within the government aid, abet, and guard Boko Haram and its activities.[91]

Saudi Arabia & Gulf States – Boko Haram received funding from organizations within Saudi Arabia and the Gulf States.[92] In addition, Yusuf sought refuge in Saudi Arabia in 2004.[93]

Aid

Weapons are often supplied through the Nigerian government, whether intentional or un-intentional. The intentional supply comes from corrupt officials in the government who agree with Boko Haram's objectives. Money and arms flow from Islamist allies within the Nigerian government.[94] The un-intentional supply comes from the military abandoning its posts and Boko Haram obtaining the weaponry in battles

Other terrorist organizations offer aid in training and weaponry (often called active support). Many organizations will offer verbal support (often called passive support) for the cause of Boko Haram.

According to International Christian Concern, Boko Haram is waging an expensive soft war (hostile acts aimed at changing society/culture). Boko Haram is largely funded by the Saudi's and Gulf States, as well as massive funding from Islamic charities.[95]

Financing

It is believed that Boko Haram relies heavily on local funding sources and criminal activity to fund itself. A large source of funding is kidnapping for ransom, which yields millions of dollars a year. The US estimates that Boko Haram receives US$1 million for each wealthy person kidnapped.[96]

It is estimated that Boko Haram secured about US$70 million between 2006 and 2011 through collaborations with organized crime syndicates and random taxation on villages. Theses syndicates operate in drug trafficking, kidnappings, bank robbery and cyber scams.[97]

Boko Haram also finances itself through bank robberies, protection money, and donations (both foreign and domestic). Donations are often from sympathizers and Islamic charities.[98]

International Sources

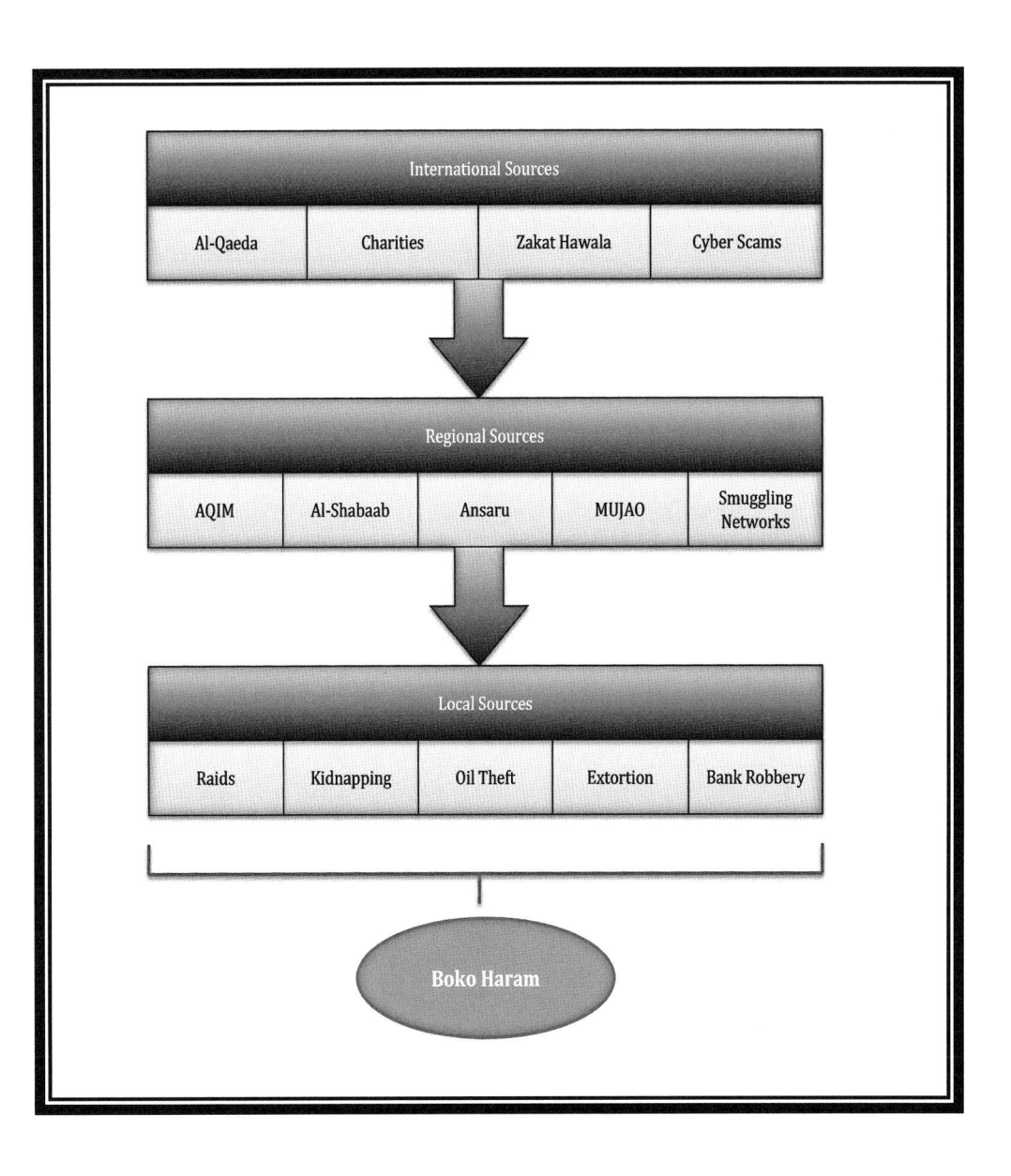

| Al-Qaeda | Charities | Zakat Hawala | Cyber Scams |

Regional Sources

| AQIM | Al-Shabaab | Ansaru | MUJAO | Smuggling Networks |

Local Sources

| Raids | Kidnapping | Oil Theft | Extortion | Bank Robbery |

Boko Haram

Tactics

Bombings

Boko Haram frequently uses bombings to further its goals. It uses vehicle-born Improvised Explosive Devices (IEDs), suicide bombers, and petrol bombs.

A tool, not new but used more frequently, in Boko Haram's arsenal has been female suicide bombers. However, unlike many other organizations, Boko Haram's female suicide bombers are accompanied by armed assaults. This allows maximum damage. While people are focused on the armed assault, the female suicide bomber (unsuspected because of her gender) can slip into a heavily populated area and detonate. Women's hijabs (long dress-like clothing) also aid in disguising the weaponry.

Using female suicide bombers also enhances Boko Haram's outreach. It shows that the group affords females opportunities just as it does males. In addition, the sheer act of the females perpetuating the violence lends a viewpoint that females are in favor of Boko Haram.

Female suicide bombers also give the group more press coverage. Incidents with bombs get a lot of media attention. If it is a suicide bomber, there is even more. But the most media attention is given to incidents with *female* suicide bombers. This is great propaganda for Boko Haram.

It has been posited that Boko Haram's switch of tactics, to incorporate women, may have been in response to the aggressive tactics of the government. In 2013, the government started pressuring Boko Haram by mass-arresting male suspects. Prior to this strategy, the government had been trying to attack Boko Haram by arresting the members' female family members. This change, to put pressure on Boko Haram by arresting men in mass, may have led to Boko Haram using women in order to be successful in its missions.[99] The extra scrutiny of men made it hard for men to be successful in their operations. Women were not being scrutinized and could pass through security measures without being detected.

Whatever the reason for using females as suicide bombers, there has been no discrimination when it comes to age. The first female bomber was middle-aged. The youngest to date has been 10 years old. This ten year old was arrested wearing a suicide belt shortly after three female recruiters were taken into custody and the military claimed Boko Haram had a "female wing" in its command structure.[100]

Other Physical Violence

Beheading, Burning, Executions, Hacking, Shooting & Throat Slitting

These are the main methods that Boko Haram uses when attacking a whole village or town. This is especially the case for revenge attacks. Most attacks involve shooting of some kind. Generally with AK-47s and heavy weaponry. Generally, houses, shops, and other buildings are burnt down. There have been instances where people have been burnt alive in their homes.

For the most part, there does not seem to be a single method preferred. It is at the discretion of those carrying out the attack and what they have available to them to use. This is a direct connection with the decentralized nature of the group. Local cells run themselves. An example would be the attack on Doron Baga in November 2014. In this instance, guns were not used as they did not want to attract the attention of the military.[101]

> *"The Boko Haram slit the throats of some of the men and tied the hands and legs of the others before throwing them into the lake to drown,"* Mr Gamandi said.[102]

Many times, multiple methods are used. An example would be the attack on Jos on December 11, 2014. There were twin bomb blasts.   Following the bombs, gunman attacked survivors. Another example would be the August 6, 2014 attack on Gwoza. Boko Haram slashed people to death and shot others to death. Then houses were fire bombed.

> "I thank God for sparing my life, but three of my neighbors and members of our church were killed during the attack," Tada said. "These Christians in our village had their throats slit with knives while their hands were tied behind their backs. Some houses were bombed as the Boko Haram gunmen were chanting, 'God is great!' in Arabic."[103]

Kidnapping

Boko Haram uses kidnapping as a way to further its means. The US believes that Boko Haram makes US$1million per wealthy individual kidnapped.[104] This is a method of financing, as well as a way to obtain other items Boko Haram deems necessary. The group also uses kidnapping as a way to control the minds and emotions of its enemies.

Boko Haram's first kidnapping was a seven-member French family in Cameroon. This abduction was followed by many more. The victims are held for monetary ransom as well as political purposes. In May 2013, 12 women and children were abducted. Shekau promised that they would become his "servants" if Boko Haram members (and their wives) were not released from prison. At this moment in the conflict between Boko Haram and Nigeria, the central strategy of the government had been to attack Boko Haram members through their female family members. This strategy may have propelled Shekau toward female-based abductions.

Female Abductions

Rich women, when abducted, yield high ransoms from their rich husbands. Women with ties to political figures can result in the release of Boko Haram members from prison. However, female abductions have evolved for Boko Haram. These are not the only targets for kidnapping. Although some women are taken arbitrarily, the majority seems to be targeted for abduction because they are/were students, Christians, or both.

Young women, if they do not yield a monetary ransom or a trade deal, are still considered good for abducting. Once abducted they are then raped, forced into marriage, and forced into conversion. Those who don't convert are subjected to physical and psychological abuse; forced labor; forced participation in military operations, including carrying ammunition or luring men into ambush; forced marriage to their captors; and sexual abuse, to include rape.[105]

> "Under sharia law, women prisoners can be taken captive. These are captives of jihad. These slaves are forced to convert to Islam and adopt their beliefs. Muhammad approved of women being taken captive for sex and ransom. This permitted having sex with Christian and Jewish women that their right hands possessed."

At times, they are also abducted for the purpose of operational support. There are reports of women being abducted in order to lure men into ambushes. They also serve as porters, carrying the loot stolen by insurgents from places they attacked. It has also been speculated that some of these abducted women are used as suicide bombers.

Abducting women and children also gives Boko Haram an emotional edge that not only keeps them in the media spotlight; it gives the group power over their adversaries. The conflict that arises over the abductions keeps the Nigerian government preoccupied, it instills fear into the villages of the abducted (which allows for confusion and sometimes acquiescence), and gives the group the edge it needs when conducting its attacks. In some instances, the threat of possibly being kidnapped helps clear people out of villages because they do not want to take the chance of being abducted.

Male Abductions
Boko Haram does abduct men and boys. They especially want men of fighting age. Men that are able to fight are often given

the choice to fight or to be killed. Boko Haram also targets men for kidnapping when the man has a skill or occupation that Boko Haram needs. This is the case for medical professionals, pharmacists, and the like.

Revenge Attacks

Revenge attacks are a very effective way for Boko Haram to control any type of resistance it may face. The few times towns and villages have attempted, sometimes successfully, to repel an attack by Boko Haram, they have been revisited with devastating consequences. On occasion, the village/town may not have even purposefully engaged in the offense, but suffer the consequences of the actions of one.

An example of this is Doron Baga. Four Boko Haram members wandered into a fish market. They were identified and killed by soldiers in a gunfight. In retaliation for this offense, Boko Haram attacked the town and slaughtered 48 people. The men either had their throats slit, or their hands and feet tied before being thrown into the nearby lake to drown. These men were likely not responsible for the Boko Haram members being identified by soldiers and subsequently killed.

Attacks such as these keep the populace afraid. When the populace is afraid, they will become more compliant, making the creation of an Islamic Caliphate inside of Nigeria within Boko Haram's grasp.

Boko Haram & Christians

Although many do not make the connection, Boko Haram is intent on killing Christians. Media often reports the killings in a non-religious fashion. However, human rights agencies and religious organizations have contacts on the ground that report otherwise.

Despite these reports, Boko Haram has clearly stated that its goal is to eradicate Christianity from Nigeria.

January 11, 2012, Abubakar Shekau stated,

> "This religion of Christianity you are practicing is not a religion of God—it is paganism. God frowns at it. What you are practicing is not religion. We are at war with Christians."[106]

In June of the same year, Abul Qaqa, a Boko Haram leader said this,

> "The Nigerian state and Christians are our enemies and we will be launching attacks on the Nigerian state and its security apparatus as well as churches until we achieve our goal of establishing an Islamic state in place of the secular state."[107]

A spokesperson for Boko Haram said this in 2012,

> "We will create so much effort to end the Christian presence in our push to have a proper Islamic state that the Christians won't be able to stay."[108]

In May 2014, Shekau reiterated his intent,

> "until we soak the ground of Nigeria with Christian blood and so-called Muslims contradicting Islam. After we have killed, killed, killed, and get fatigued and wonder what to do with smelling of their corpses – smelling of Obama, Bush and Goodluck Jonathan – then we will open prison and imprison the rest. Infidels have no value."

In December 2014, a leader of Boko Haram sent out a video showing a mass execution. In the video he states,

> "We have made sure the floor of this hall is turned red with blood, and this is how it is going to be in all future attacks and arrests of infidels. From now, killing, slaughtering, destructions and bombing will be our religious duty anywhere we invade."[109]

Samuel Kunhiyop, a leading Nigerian Evangelical gave even more insight into this issue while interviewing with Christianity Today.[110]

Are Christians being targeted? Or are these attacks possibly reprisals against the government or civilized activity of any kind?

"Boko Haram is an extremist Islamic organization. In 1992, the Islamic community expressed its desire, along with the Organization of Islamic Conference (OIC), to make all of Nigeria a Muslim state. [Nigeria is an OIC member.] Over 90 percent of buildings destroyed by Boko Haram are Christian churches.

But the church in the north is strong and vibrant. Boko Haram wants to eliminate the churches because they are unacceptable to Muslims. They don't want Christians in the Muslim areas, so they bomb those places of worship, or refuse to give them a license to worship."

Is Nigeria as bad as we read in news headlines?

"It's even worse. Hundreds of churches have been destroyed, over 50 in Kano alone. One church and ministry has been built seven times and destroyed seven times. Another has been built three times and destroyed three times. Pastors have been murdered in their houses. Another was murdered in the church during a prayer service.

The situation is much worse further north in Yobe and Borno states, the headquarters of Boko Haram. People have fled residences where their forefathers lived for generations. Christians have been the victims."

Killing & Injuring

Obtaining accurate numbers in Nigeria is challenging to everyone. Communication towers are often destroyed by Boko Haram, villages can be very remote making it hard to get information, the chaotic situations can be difficult to see through, and many times organizations must rely on witness testimony. An example of this difficulty can be seen in the attack on Gwoza on August 6, 2014.

Caused by Boko Haram	2014
Christians Kidnapped	771+
Christians Killed	3,043+
Houses Burned	225+
Churches Burned	41+

On August 6, 2014, Boko Haram attacked the town of Gwoza. Reports from that day, and there were many, put the death toll around 100 (no less than 90 and no more than 103). As it is extremely difficult to get information from towns that are completely destroyed and taken over by Boko Haram, these were the best numbers. News media focused on the number 100, it was a nice number in the middle. It could be expected that there might be an additional 10 or 20 victims that died trying to escape and their bodies were not yet found. But it wasn't 10 or 20, there were 900 more.

On August 13, a week after the attack, Ojutiku, a Nigerian relations expert, got a message from a trusted colleague in

Gwoza. A woman burying the bodies of all the victims has a different number.

> *"The terrorists seized a number of residents as hostages and killed nine hundred and ninety seven...bodies confirmed. The insurgents took over the Emirs Palace as well as a Government Lodge and have appointed a replacement for the town's fleeing Emir. They have hoisted their black flags with Arabic insignia all over Gwoza in a show of their total control of the territory."*

This incident is a perfect example of how hard it can be to calculate total numbers for anything. The media did not pick up on this report. Most agencies will likely be using the 100 number. In addition, we may have figured out that more died, but there are no numbers on the injured. Many do not report to hospitals, are seeking safety in the wilderness, or are hiding their injuries. Most are happy to be alive and do not report.

> "So, when you meet (in fight jihad in Allah's Cause), those who disbelieve smite at their necks till when you have killed and wounded many of them, then bind a bond firmly (on them, i.e. take them as captives)...Thus [you are ordered by Allah to continue in carrying out jihad against the disbelievers till they embrace Islam], but if it had been Allah's will, He Himself could certainly have punished them (without you). But (He lets you fight), in order to test you, some with others. But those who are killed in the Way of Allah, He will never let their deeds be lost.
> Quran 47:4"

In its efforts to rid Nigeria of Christians, Boko Haram focuses its attacks on churches as well as villages and towns that are known to be Christian or have a Christian majority. This can make ascertaining religion-based killings a little difficult.

When churches are attacked, or locals clearly identify the dead being Christian, it is easy to see the motivations of Boko Haram. However, many times whole villages are razed to the ground and any survivors flee into the bush. Thus, reporting does not indicate that the attack was based upon religion.

For 2014, 4,733 deaths by Boko Haram were Christians or unspecified people. Boko Haram is responsible for many military and police deaths and Muslim deaths (as can be seen in the mosque bombing and the threatening of the Emir of Kano). The military and police are killed in clashes with Boko Haram. The attacks targeting Muslims happen because Boko Haram sees them as siding with infidels in some capacity.

The 4,733 deaths include Christians and victims that were left unspecified. This number is likely low. Many villages cannot get the word out about what has happened to them. Oftentimes, information gleaned is inaccurate because of the chaotic situation. Out of this total, 3,043 were designated Christian. They were targeted while worshipping in their church, because of their personal belief, or because their town was Christian dominated. The rest of that figure are people who's religion and/or government affiliation is unknown. They are not targeted for their moderate Islamic belief, because they are military/police, or because of their political affiliation. Those motivations are usually very clear in reporting and were taken out of the assessment. Therefore, these unknowns are likely Christians.

It should be noted that the total of 3,043 <u>Christian</u> deaths by Boko Haram is almost twice the number of <u>total</u> deaths by Boko Haram in 2013.

Kidnapping
In 2014, there were 991 people, either Christians or undesignated, kidnapped in Nigeria by Boko Haram in 17 different attacks. This number is likely higher as many reports did not have exact numbers (i.e. – reported "dozens" or "many") and the media is not always made aware of a kidnapping due to communication issues within Nigeria. Also, for the purposes of this book, any incident that was specifically outlined to be against a target that was not Christian (i.e. – Muslim, government, etc.), was not included in the statistics.

So the <u>total</u> number of kidnappings for Boko Haram is much higher.

Out of the 17 attacks, 7 were confirmed to be targeting Christians. That is a total of 771 people that were kidnapped because of their Christian beliefs. That leaves 220 people that were kidnapped and the motive is unknown. It is likely that these remaining victims are also Christians as politically motivated and Islam-related kidnappings are reported as such. That leaves no other motivation except anti-Christian sentiments.

It is possible that there are other motives for the kidnappings, however history dictates that Boko Haram kidnaps for three reasons:

1) Ransom Money
2) Politics
3) Anti-Christian

Those kidnapped for ransom are wealthy or have wealthy connections. Because of this, the kidnappings are reported as such. Boko Haram makes demands and the media catches wind of these demands. These victims are not kidnapped because of anything other than the money they can bring to Boko Haram. This is the case with the 2013 kidnapping of a French family. Because kidnapping for ransom generates a demand for money, the unknown kidnappings cannot be money related.

Boko Haram also targets government officials and people with political influence for kidnapping. These kidnappings allow Boko Haram to demand the release of their imprisoned members and engage in extortion. Those with connections can get Boko Haram what they want. So they are targeted with that in mind. Because a kidnapping in relation to politics also generates a demand for something, the unknown kidnappings cannot fall into this category.

Lastly, Boko Haram targets Christians, specifically girls but not always, in order to force them to convert, marry them off, use them as slaves, and to help support operations. The group targets the Christians because they hate Christians.

There are instances of Islamic girls being kidnapped. However, it is generally the case that they are collateral damage. This is the case with the Chibok schoolgirl kidnapping. Over 90% of the girls kidnapped were Christians. The school was targeted because it was a school and because it was where most of the Christians went to school. The Muslim girls that got kidnapped were done so by accident. In addition, there are many reports of the Boko Haram members separating Christians from Muslims before they engage in their attack.

In addition, Human Rights Watch has found that in regards to abducted women and girls, the majority appeared to have been targeted for abduction because they were students, Christians, or both.[111]

Therefore, it stands to reason that unless Boko Haram states otherwise, any kidnapping that takes place, should fall into the three motives that Boko Haram has for kidnapping. Because kidnapping for ransom and politics is always reported with a motive as such, it can be ascertained that the kidnappings that have no motive attached to them are likely to be of Christians.

News Stories & Witness Accounts

This section is by no means exhaustive. However, in order to fully appreciate what is going on in any situation, accounts by people who have lived it are necessary. In this section you will find a few cases that have been covered by worldwide media, as well as witness accounts. These serve to show the side of things that facts and data cannot. It is an insight into the constant struggle and the continual obstacles that many face in Nigeria.

These stories are reports by news agencies, NGOs, Congress, and religious organizations. The citations provide the location of the full report. Often, English is a second language to these survivors and the grammar is not always correct. Because the testimony is about them and their experience in their own words, everything was left as it was. It was not changed.

Because the stories are so numerous, they cannot all be accounted for in this book. In addition, the overall meaning is often lost if too much time is spent in the horrific details. It only takes one example of a beheading to understand the horrific nature of the action. Therefore, no more than one account is needed. Hopefully, these chosen stories will help you get into the minds, the feelings, and the lives of Christians in Nigeria.

Woman from Izghe[112]
An 18-year-old woman explained why she fled her village. She is just one of many displaced from her village.

"My mother told me to run from our village to another town though we know no one here, because of the scary rate of abductions of young women, including married ones. In February my brother's 16-year-old wife was abducted with their two children and they have not been fount 'til date. The insurgents returned a month later to kill my other brother and took away his teenage wife but left her young baby behind. She managed to escape from the insurgents' camp and is back home now mourning her murdered husband. My mother became afraid that I would be the next target so she sent me away. I have been sleeping in a church since I arrived in this town a few days ago."

Accounts from Kidnapped Girls
Girl #1 "They told the Muslims to stand to one side, and the four of us Christians to the other. They released the Muslims but kept us."

They were then raped and told not to talk to the media when they were returned home.[113]

Girl #2 She was forced to go on operations with the insurgents and carried their bullets. At one time, they tried to make her kill a man. She was unable to do so and fell to the ground. They forced her to watch them kill a man. She eventually escaped by pretending to have stomach pains. They sent her to the hospital and she was able to escape from there.

"My dreams are filled with regret for renouncing my religion instead of enduring the abuse of the insurgents. Even when I'm awake, I'm upset about the situation."[114]

Female #1 "One young woman held in a camp near Gwoza described how combatants placed a noose around her neck and threatened her with death until she renounced her religion; others were repeatedly threatened with whipping, beating, or death unless they converted to Islam, stopped attending school, and complied with Islamic dressing rules, such as wearing veils or hijab."[115]

Female #2 Originally, she cooked for a group of 14 men. She was soon in the fighting as Boko Haram forced her to carry their bullets during operations. Eventually, she was ordered to approach members of the Civilian Joint Task Force. Afraid because of all she had seen the insurgents do, she pretended to need their help. They followed her into an ambush.

"Once we got back to the camp, they tied the legs and hands of the captives and slit the throats of four of them as they shouted 'Allahu Akbar.' Then I was handed a knife to kill the last man. I was shaking with horror and couldn't do it. The camp leader's wife took the knife and killed him."[116]

Female #3 "I was lying down in the cave pretending to be ill because I did not want the marriage the commander planned to conduct for me with another insurgent on his return from the Sambisa camp. When the insurgent who had paid my dowry came in to force himself on me, the commander's wife blocked the cave entrance and watched as the man raped me."[117]

Patience[118]
Age: 18 years

The 18-year-old high school student escaped from Boko Haram with her life, but she's feeling sharp loss.

One of more than 300 girls kidnapped by the Islamic extremist group on April 15 from Government Girls Secondary School in Chibok, in Nigeria's northeastern state of Borno, Patience (last name withheld for security reasons) indicated she is deeply troubled by the captivity of her best friend and others.

"I have lost all my books, clothing and other valuables," she said of the Boko Haram raid that began late at night on April 14. "But all these are not important now. I miss all my friends and schoolmates and will like to plead with the gunmen to release them."

A member of the Church of the Brethren in Nigeria (EYN), Patience was one of 57 girls who escaped after Boko Haram rebels, who seek to establish a strict version of sharia (Islamic law) throughout Nigeria, herded the girls, most of them Christians, onto trucks at gunpoint.

"They wore military camouflage, and we thought they were soldiers who had come to assist us, but we later realized that they were Boko Haram gunmen," she told Morning Star News. "Having set fire on the school buildings, they moved us to under a big locust bean tree and forced us to enter some trucks they brought with them. They asked us all to either enter the trucks or we get killed. We were all scared and had to enter the vehicles."

After about 30 minutes, three of the nine trucks began to break down, she said. They tried to force the girls from the faulty trucks onto the others and set the three broken ones ablaze, but those in the overflow were forced to walk alongside the convoy.

"They [Boko Haram] moved on with us until we got to a village there in the bush, where they stopped," Patience said. "Our colleagues who were forced to trek had meanwhile covered more than 20 kilometers [12 miles] on foot."

When the vehicles stopped, Patience decided to make her move.

"I jumped out of the vehicle and hid myself under a thorn bush close by the vehicle tracks," she said. "When I jumped out of the vehicle, I could no longer move my legs as I was injured. So, I dragged myself on my stomach and hid under a thorn bush."

Following her lead, her friend Parmata also jumped out of the truck. Because of the noise of the trucks, Patience was able to call out to her unnoticed, and under cover of darkness her friend was able to run and join her under the bush.

"We saw the gunmen pass the thorn bush where we hid ourselves, but they could not see us," Patience said. "We hid ourselves under the thorn bush until daybreak at about 6 a.m., when my friend decided to move out to find help since I was unable to walk because of my injured legs."

At length her friend chanced upon a nomadic ethnic Fulani cattleman.

"The Fulani man brought his bicycle and carried me on it, while my friend trekked along until we finally met with some parents from Chibok who had been in search of us," Patience said. "And one of the parents from Chibok who had a motorbike was asked by others with him to convey me and my friend back to Chibok, while the other parents continued on the trail of the Boko Haram gunmen."

She named several classmates and friends still captive, adding that most did not appear in a video recently released by Boko Haram.

"I saw only two of these my friends in the video recently made public by Boko Haram," she said. "But some of the faces I saw in the video clip were not known to me, even though there were others that were our schoolmates that I could recognize."

While members of her church came to her house to pray for her and her family, and the church has assisted with some funds, no other organization has offered assistance, Patience said.

"Not even my local government officials, Borno state government, National Emergency Management Authority or the police have assisted in any way," she said.

While the students at the school who escaped were soon called to take their final tests – exams being the reason the school was open at the time of the attack, as the government had closed other schools following Boko Haram threats – Patience said she was saddened that her leg injuries kept her from doing so.

"My mother had to foot my medical bills," she added. Patience, who traveled to Abuja with her brother to meet with Morning Star News and a U.S. delegation, has not received adequate medical care, but she did not appear concerned about herself.

"Please, Boko Haram people, my appeal is that you release my friends and schoolmates and let them return to their parents," she said.

Chibok Kidnappings

Saa – Escaped Boko Haram[119]
Saa was loaded into a truck when she became overcome with fear and tried to make a run for it. "I told my friend that I

decided to jump down from the truck. I'd rather die, that my parents [would] have my coffin buried than to go with them because we don't know where we are going."

She and her friend jumped out of the truck and fled into the forest. They spent one night under a tree and managed to get help. They were ultimately reunited with their families.

"I'm a Christian, I'm a real Christian. I know God, and I'm following God the way I can."

Parent of Two Daughters Still Abducted[120]
"I find it difficult to eat or sleep. How can I when my daughters are probably sleeping out in the open exposed to all kinds of danger? My wife looks at me sorrowfully as if I should be able to do something. She is sick, but I know it is only worry and heartache. If even the soldiers are afraid of these militants, how can we civilians confront them? The worst part of it is that no one is telling us anything. We try to gather information from other towns, but what we hear gives us no hope. Why can't the government help us or tell us what they are doing to get our daughters back? I am tired of living like this."

Congressional Testimony of Deborah Peters[121]
My name is Deborah Peter and I am the sole survivor of a Boko Haram attack on my household.

On December 22, 2011 at 7pm, my brother and I were at home when we started hearing some guns shooting. My brother called my dad and told him not to come home because some people were shooting guns. But my dad said he should not worry because it was not the first time he had come home when people were fighting. When my dad came home, he said that he was going to take a shower because he was hot.

At 7:30pm, three men knocked on the door. My brother answered the door because he recognized one of the men as a Muslim in our community. The men asked where my dad was and I told them that he was in the shower. The men waited.

After three minutes, they went into the bathroom and dragged my dad into the main room. They said that my dad was wasting their time and that they did not have time to wait on him. The men told my dad that he should deny his Christian faith. My dad told them that he would not deny his faith. They said that if he did not deny his faith they were going to kill him. My dad refused, saying that Jesus said whoever acknowledges Him in front of man, He will acknowledge in front of Godl; and whoever denies Him in front of man, He will deny in front of God in heaven. My dad said that he would rather die than go to hell fire. After he told the men that, the men shot him three times in his chest.

My brother was in shock. He started demanding, "What did my dad do to you? Why did you shoot him?" The men told him to be quiet or else they were going to shoot him too. Then, the men discussed whether they should kill y brother. One of the Boko Harams said they should kill Caleb, my brother. The second man said that he was just a boy and that he was too young to kill. But the third man said that they should make an exception in this case because Caleb will only grow up to be a Christian pastor. Caleb asked me to plead with them for his life but they told me to shut up or they would kill me too. The leader agreed that they should kill him and shot my brother two times. My dad had still been breathing but when he saw them shoot Caleb, he died.

My brother fell down but was still alive and gasping. The men shot him in his mouth. Then, my brother stopped moving and died. I was in shock. I did not know what was happening. The men put me in the middle of my dad and brother's corpses, told me to be quiet or be killed, and left me there. I stayed there until the next day when the army came. They removed my dad and brother's bodies to the mortuary and took me to the hospital.

I was traumatized. A nearby pastor paid for me to get out of town when he discovered that Boko Haram said they made a mistake by not also killing me. Boko Haram decided later that they should have killed me because I am the daughter of an apostate Muslim mother who converted to Christianity. So the pastor paid for me to get out of that region. I fled and Jubilee Campaign helped me come to a 9/11 child survivors of terrorism camp in America. On May 15, 2013, that pastor, Rev Faye Pama, was killed by Boko Haram in front of his kids.

Similar to that pastor, my family was targeted by Boko Haram because we are Christians. My dad was a pastor. We had to move from place to place because Boko Haram always attacked my father and told him that they would kill him. In November, they burned his church and threatened him. My dad refused to deny his faith and rebuilt his church. That is why they killed him - because he is a Christian.

I decided to tell the world my story when the Chibok girls were taken because everyone needs to know how horrible Boko Haram is. They kill innocent people who never hurt them. I want the world to understand what happened to me. I hope that the kidnapped Chibok girls will take courage from my story, and know more of what God says, and know what it means to stand strong in the face of bad people. I hope that they will be free and be able to go to school and worship freely. I hope that like me, some of them can come and continue their education America.

My mum graduated from the school from which they were kidnapped. Chibok is a small town where everyone is related to everyone else and although it is majority Christian, everyone lived in peace until Boko Haram came. I know at least one of the kidnapped schoolgirls name Hauwa. I pray for them and ask everyone to pray for them too.

I am thankful to Tuesday's Children, the 911 Foundation for inviting me to a summer camp for child survivors of terrorism, I am thankful to Jubilee Campaign for bringing me to America and I am thankful to Mt Mission School for giving me a chance to continue my education and being a home to me in America.

Executed or Not?[122]

Boko Haram violence has increased in number and force since 2009 after it developed ties with Al Qaeda in the Islamic Mahgreb (AQIM). A 29-year-old Christian in Kauri, Borno state who felt the force of Boko Harm weaponry in December 2012 said he would invite his assailants to dine with him.

A married father of three children ages 7, 5 and 1, Ayuba (surname withheld) told Morning Star News he has forgiven the gunmen who shot him three times.

"Despite my ordeal at the hands of these Boko Haram gunmen, I want to assure you that I hold no grudges against them," he said. "If I see any of them today, I will still welcome them to my house and feed them. Jesus Christ, our Lord, taught us to love those who hate us."

Ayuba and his wife were working on their farm in the village of Mainari, on the fringes of the Sambisa Forest in Borno state, on Dec. 20, 2012, when he returned to his house to rest. He was surprised to find two motorcycles parked beside his house, he said.

"I parked my motorcycle outside the house too, and then went inside, and just then I heard movement outside the house," he said.

He went out to find two armed Boko Haram members; they asked him his name. When he told them, they asked if it was true that he was a Christian. A member of the Church of Christ in Nations (COCIN), he responded that he was.

"From their utterances I knew that they must have gotten detailed information about me from our Muslim neighbors in Mainari village," he said. "Having confirmed I was the person they were looking for, they told that my end had come. 'You have refused to become a Muslim in spite of all pressure from our Muslim brothers here,' one of them told me. 'You have refused to renounce your faith in Jesus. So, we have no option than to kill you.'"

He then recalled that Muslims in Kauri twice had tried to convert him.

"I braced up and asked the gunmen why they want to kill me simply because I am a Christian, and the second among the two gunmen told me that, 'You are an infidel, and we do not want to have infidels living among us here.'"

They demanded money and the keys to his motorbike. After forcefully taking the keys to his vehicle and removing 35,000 naira (US$212) from his pocket, they told him to lie down because they were going to shoot him, he said.

"Instead of obeying their instructions, I started praying," he said. "They became angry because I was praying out loud and calling on the name of Jesus. They shoved me in an effort to force me down to the ground. Eventually they succeeded in forcing me to the ground, and then one of them ordered his colleague to shoot me."

He heard a gunshot, and a bullet pierced his left hand, which he had used to cover his chest, he said. A second shot aimed at his stomach, which he was covering with his right hand. The bullet pierced his right hand.

"To the surprise of the gunmen, they found I was still alive and praying," he said. "The gunman who gave the orders that I should be shot was angry that his colleague did not kill me in spite of two point-blank gunshots."

The one who had given the orders angrily cocked his gun and shot at his forehead, he said.

"One experience I will not forget throughout my life is that the bullet from the third shot hit me on my forehead and bounced to hit me on my right shoulder, instead of penetrating through my skull," he said. "To me, this is a miracle, as I cannot explain how three shots were fired at me at point-blank range, yet I was still alive."

The two Boko Haram gunmen took him for dead as they rode away, he said.

"After about an hour, my wife returned to find me on the spot where I was shot," he said. "I still could talk, but the state she saw me in was shocking to her, so she began to cry."

He asked her to search for help, which did not arrive until five hours later. He had been shot at about 3 p.m., and a neighbor his wife found came to help him at 8 p.m., he said. He was taken first to Kauri, then to General Hospital in Konduga. Doctors treating him there advised that he be taken away lest the Boko Haram gunmen trace him and kill him at the hospital.

His wife and other relatives moved him to Adventist Hospital at Kozat, Cameroon, where he remained for three months before going to an undisclosed town.

Boko Haram has destroyed his COCIN church building in Kauri, he said, and all Christians there have fled.

"Some of our church members died in the attack by Boko Haram gunmen, while others were forced to flee to Cameroon, where they are now refugees," he said. "I have been praying that these Boko Haram gunmen will eventually get to know Jesus, repent of their crimes against the church, and become the followers of Jesus."

Forced Marriages
Abubakar Shekau, in a video, boasted that the Chibok students would be given in marriage to his group members: "We would also give their hands in marriage because they are our slaves. We would marry them out at the age of nine. We would marry them out at the age of 12."[123]

"When one of the girls, a 17-year-old farmer, complained to a Boko Haram commander that they were too young for marriage, he pointed at this 5-year-old daughter and said: 'If she got married last year, and is just waiting till puberty for its consummation, how can you at your age be too young to marry?'"[124]

Gajiganna Village[125]

"They preside over meetings in most of the villages, execute judgement for the people and police most of the communities. Just before they attacked Gajigana, they have been coming around to judge the people. In fact, about one week to the attack, there was problem between one of our friends and a Fulani man who put his cows in the farm; we had to report the matter to them (Boko Haram); they came and gave the Fulani man one day for him to pay compensation; he agreed and paid amount equivalent to five bags of beans," he disclosed.

"In a form of reprisal, members of the Boko Haram now attacked Gajiganna, because they believed that those that reported them to soldiers were from the area. They took some people and killed them. When we thought that it was over, they suddenly decided to start burning houses," he further disclosed.

"Whatever you are doing, they watch you; they monitor every movement," he said.

Grave Digger[126]

At 35 years of age, this woman became a de facto grave digger. Boko Haram often kills all the men, slaughters them, and then leaves the bodies to rot. Women and children are left behind to mourn and clean up bodies; something that in their culture, women are not allowed to do.

After Boko Haram attacked her village, killing all the men, the women hid where they could. When the stench of decomposing bodies of their loved ones was too much to bear, the women came out to bury their dead, despite the cultural taboos of doing so. To the best of their ability, the women gave their families and fellow villagers a befitting burial, despite the fact they could not dig deep enough graves.

After personally burying 40 bodies, badly decomposed, she could handle no more and fled to another village.

Before the attack, she had her own businesses and was doing pretty well. A mother of five, she was happy. But that all came crumbling down after the attack. She now lives hand to mouth, having lost everything except her children.

Jummai Sunday[127]
Age: 63 years
Date of Death: December 11, 2014

Jummai was a devoted Christian woman. Even always loved and served others. Even when times were tough, Jummai still gave food to those without. She visited others, praying with them, consoling those that were mourning, and sharing Scripture with those she thought needed it.

"Sometimes she would abandon her wares in the market and go out to share the Word of God with others before returning to the market," her daughter said. "There were times I had to talk to her to minimize her zeal for outreach to others, but she would caution me and say she is into the business of winning souls for God and not looking for money."

December 11th was no different until Boko Haram entered the market. After a morning devotional, Jummai visited sick/bereaved families and then returned to her home to gather items for her market spot in Jos, Nigeria. It was that night that twin bomb blasts by Boko Haram swept through the market. She survived. Barely. 31 others didn't, including her son and sister.

As she scrambled to get away, gunmen who were targeting survivors shot Jummai in the head, leg and hand. She was taken to a hospital in the Muslim quarter of the city. It wasn't long before a Muslim found Jummai's cell phone and called her daughter.

It was close to midnight. The caller told her that Jummai was in the hospital and was so critical that she could not talk on the phone. They hung up. It wasn't long and that Muslim called back, warning her not to go to the hospital as Muslims in the area were attacking and killing Christians. She called her brother.

Jummai's son, accompanied by police and soldiers, went to the hospital, but Jummai had not survived.

Join or Die[128]

"The blockade was up to 40 vehicles long. When the men in military uniform separated the Muslims from the Christians, we knew then they were Boko Haram. All young men including Muslims were told to either join the insurgents or be killed. They slit the throat of some of the men, saying they'd not waste bullets on them. Christian women wearing pants were shot in the leg and left to die. Older Muslim men and women wearing Muslim veils were released to go, while the rest of us were driven to their camp in Sambisa forest."

Slaughtered and Lived[129]

Adamu, 28, bears a scar on the back of his neck where two members of the Islamic extremist group Boko Harm tried to slaughter him.

A member of the Church of the Brethren in Nigeria (EYN) in Gwoza, Borno state in northeastern Nigeria, Adamu told Morning Star News that in April 2013 he was working on his bean farm in Musari village, in the Mungono area, when a member of the insurgent Boko Haram approached him.

"He told me to convert to Islam and join them in waging a jihad to establish an Islamic state in Nigeria," said Adamu, whose surname is withheld for security reasons. "I told him that I will not renounce my Christian faith in order to embrace Islam. He left me there on my farm without saying anything again."

Two days later, five other members of Boko Haram showed up. The insurgency is fighting to impose strict sharia (Islamic law) throughout Nigeria.

"They said their member told them that I refused to renounce being a Christian and wanted to know whether it is true that I refused to become a Muslim," Adamu said, adding that he told them it was true. "They then told me that since I refused to recant, they would kill me."

When he refused their order to lie down, they seized him and tied his hands and legs behind his back, he said.

"They pinned me down and told me they will make death painful and slow, as they are not prepared to waste their bullets on me," he said. "They also said they would not give me the honor of slaughtering me by cutting my neck from the front, because that is the way they slaughter their rams.

"They forced me down on my stomach and then proceeded to slaughter me by cutting my neck from the back. I was bleeding and went blank as the knife cut through my neck. It was pains I cannot explain to you. After cutting my neck, they left me bleeding."

Adamu lay there for days, he said, adding that his survival was miraculous; only later would he learn that the Boko Haram members had threatened to kill anyone in the village who helped him.

"It was only after I was taken to the hospital that I was told that the Boko Haram members who attacked me on the farm had gone to the village shortly after leaving me bleeding to death and had warned other Muslims that if any of them dares to rescue me, he would be killed," he said. "They sternly warned other Muslims in Musari, 'We have butchered an infidel there on his farm. Be warned that if any of you Muslims dares to assist him, he is also an infidel and we shall make sure that he too is killed."

Though the villagers were afraid to rescue him, eventually a member of his church snuck onto the farm and found him alive, he said.

"He went back to the village and mobilized some of our church members who came to the farm and took me away," Adamu said.

They took him to a Christian hospital in Cameroon.

"I was taken to Adventist Hospital, Koza, in Cameroon, and treated for three months before I was referred to this hospital here in Jos," Adamu said. "The cut on my neck, doctors say, has affected some nerves and veins in my body, thereby making it difficult for me to move my limbs. Right now, I am still learning how to move my hands and legs."

Adamu said that before the attack on his farm, Boko Harm destroyed his EYN church building in Musari, and all Christians there fled.

"As I talk to you, there are no more Christians in Musari village," he said. "They attacked Christians and destroyed the church building where we worship. Our pastor and other Christians, about 120 of them, were forced to flee."

Congressional Testimony of Habila Adamu Nov 13, 2013[130]
On November 28, 2012, gunmen came to my home at around 11 p.m. and confronted me with my family. I thought they were

soldiers on patrol, and when they opened the door, I was shocked to see that they were wearing robes and masks.

The gunmen ordered me to come out with my family. And when I came out, they ordered my family to go back, and my wife begged them not to harm me. They said she should go back, because they were here to do the work of Allah. When I heard that, I knew that they were here to kill me.

And my wife brought money to them and begged them not to harm me, they collected the money and they also collected our cell phones. They asked me for the key of the door, and I gave it. One of them opened the door another two more people come inside, making them four in my house with Ak47.

They asked for my name and I told them, Habila Adamu. They asked if I am a member of Nigeria Police, I said no. Are you a Nigeria soldier? I said no. You are a member of the state security service (SSS), I said no, I told them that I am a business man.

"Okay, are you a Christian?" I said I am a Christian. They asked me why are we preaching the message of Mohammed to you and you refuse to accept Islam.

I told them I am a Christian, we are also preaching the gospel of true God to you and other people that are not yet to know God. They asked me if I mean we Christian know God. And I told them we know God and that is why I preach the good news to other people that do not know God.

Then they asked me, "Habila, are you ready to die as a Christian?' I told them, "I am ready to die as a Christian." For the second time, they asked me, "Are you ready to die as a Christian?" and I told them, 'I am ready," but before I closed my mouth, they have fired me through my nose and the bullet came out through the back. I fell on the ground. The gunmen thought I was already dead because they stomped on me two times and discovered I was dead, and cried out "Allah Akbar."

Also my wife thought I was dead, she is crying, while crying she said many things, she said let God give her the heart that she can stand to the end like what I did, let God give my children the heart that they may stand in their faith. When she continues saying all those things, I told her that I am alive. She said that but even though you are alive, the way you are bleeding, you will not survive. And I told her that even though I will die I have a message to everyone that will hear my story after I leave this world that "to live in this world is to live for Christ, to die is a gain" that is my message. I asked her to look for help. And she went out; she found out that our Christian neighbors have been killed. We have one elder in my church, himself and his son were killed that night, including twelve others.

I was on the ground from 11pm til 7am in the morning, bleeding. In the morning my face was swollen, my eyes were red. Before morning I could not see anything, around 7am I was rushed to hospital in Potiskum, for medication, from then they transferred me to Jos University Hospital same day. I am alive because God want you to have a message. I have a message, just as I told my wife as I was left for dead, I have a message to everyone that will hear my story. Do everything that you can to end this ruthless religious persecution in Northern Nigeria. My friends knowing Christ are deeper, than hearing of his name or knowing his story.

I also like to express my appreciation to God almighty and the Voice of Christian Martyrs for their supports, in standing by my side throughout, they paid for my operation, and paid for my housing, they paid for my feeding, etc. Let God bless them abundantly.

Children's Bible
Source: Stephens Children Home and Voice of the Christian Martyrs Nigeria[131]

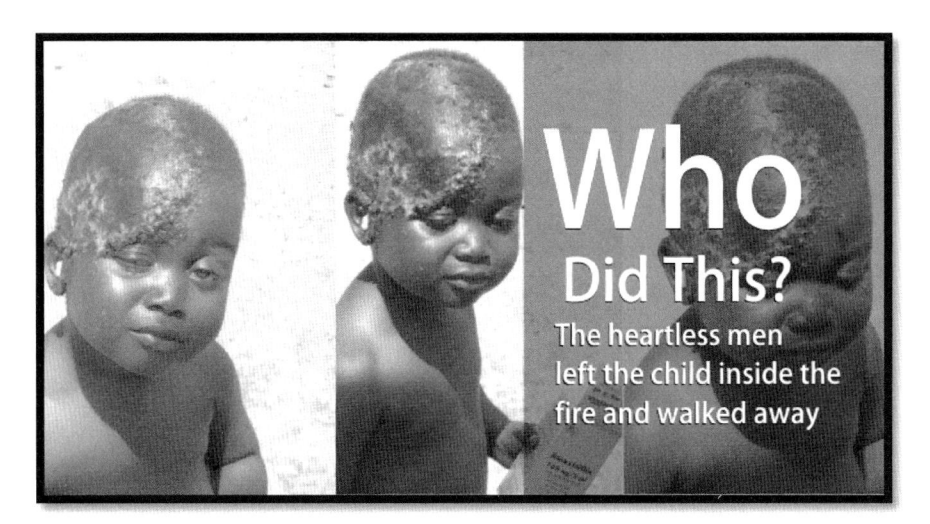

After a brutal attack on Christian worshippers on Sunday, November 22 in Attagara, Hassan was running back home holding his 'Children's Bible' when three Islamic insurgents grabbed him and sat him down.

According to an eyewitness, one of the insurgents wanted to take the Children's Bible from Hassan's hand but the little boy refused. The Muslim insurgent snatched the Bible by force and threw it into a nearby burning fire. Hassan ran to where the fire was to rescue his Bible.

While he was struggling with a stick to remove his Bible from the fire, an insurgent hit three-year-old Hassan on the head with the butt of an AK47 and pushed the little child into the fire. Not satisfied, he proceed to step on Hassan's head and pressed the head of the child into the fire, all the while railing curses and abuses on the boy and calling him 'stubborn infidel.'

The heartless Muslim left Hassan and walked away.

Hassan survived the attack but was badly burned.

Boko Haram's Caliphate

Boko Haram wants to install an Islamic Caliphate within Nigeria. Strict Sharia law would be used to govern it. Hands would be cut off for stealing, you could be killed for adultery, non-Muslims would be subjugated, and Christians and Jews would be killed. The living conditions under this type of rule would be a violation of human rights at a minimum and getting to this point will be nothing short of genocide.

Kalli Abdullah, resident of Gajiganna, who escaped to Maiduguri, said this about the living conditions of his town, which was taken over by Boko Haram,

> "They monitor every movement, all the things we do, the kind of people you meet with and sometimes they would call you to ask what you discussed or what you heard people discussing. If you lie in your response and they find out, they will get you and kill you so as to instill fear in the people, who will then tell them everything they know."[132]

Currently, there are 12 local government councils of Borno state that are under the control of Boko Haram – Abadam, Kukawa, Mart Ngala, Dikwa, Mobbar, Nganzai, Magumeri, Marte, Kala-Balge, and Monguo.[133] In December 2014, the Nigerian army uncovered plans to attack 25 communities and villages across five different states. The five states were identified as Adamawa, Borno, Bauchi, Gombe, and Yobe. Although the five states were identified, the military did not release the names of the 25 towns. A security source said,

> "You know that people would begin to fell the areas once they hear anything. I can tell you that not even one person would be left in the places If you mention the names: and that is unnecessary now."[134]

Because Boko Haram is so intent on creating its own caliphate, it has spread its violence to include anyone who would stand against them. In December 2014, Shekau released a video threatening the Emir of Kano (a high ranking Muslim). This was shortly after 120 Muslims were killed by a bomb.

This change in tactic is directly influenced by the belief that Shekau's extremist views are the only true way of Islam. Islamic State ideology and methods have likely influenced this way of thinking that allows for the killing of fellow Muslims who stand in the way of instilling an Islamic Caliphate.

Boko Haram & Genocide

In its efforts to create a Sharia-run Islamic Caliphate, Boko Haram has pointedly targeted Christians. Through the words of its adherents and through the actions it perpetrates, Boko Haram is engaging in the deliberate and systematic extermination of Christians within Nigeria.

For genocide to be declared, one of five conditions has to be met. Boko Haram has to have the intent to destroy, in whole or part, Christians.

Killing members of the group

As evidenced, Boko Haram has killed 3,043 Christians, at a *minimum*, which is twice the amount of all people killed by Boko Haram in 2013. This is a fact. But that is not where this ends. Boko Haram has declared a war on Christians and promises to bring about the annihilation of Christians in Nigeria. It's *intent* is to completely destroy Christianity within Nigeria and the surrounding countries.

These facts alone convict Boko Haram of genocide. However, Boko Haram is guilty of much more.

Causing serious bodily or mental harm to members of the group

The number of reported Christian injuries is incalculable because of the lack of reporting. Mental damage (trauma, depression, suicide, insomnia, etc) is not reported at all, but physical injuries also go unreported. Hospitals, NGO's, and religious organizations attempt to capture the amount of injuries through witness accounts, government reporting, and hospital admissions. However, many do not admit themselves into the hospital or go to the police to report an incident. Many just flee into the wilderness and take care of their own injuries.

It can be assumed that for most attacks, there are significantly more injured than dead. In addition, those that are displaced can be construed as being injured just due to the fact that they are no longer able to go home, if there home is even still standing. Human rights organizations put the number of displaced over 1 million.[135]

Boko Haram frequently razes villages to the ground. Houses and churches are main targets for burning, sometimes with people in them. It is uncommon for the media to track damage to houses and churches. When it is reported, it is often done so with words like "several" or "many" instead of numbers. Because damage is so extensive, and those reporting are focused on casualty numbers, the amount of damage done to houses and churches is substantially underreported. For 2014, **minimums** of 225 houses were razed and 41 churches were burnt to the ground.

There can be no question between the data available and the witness accounts that Boko Haram causes significant bodily and mental harm to Christians.

Deliberately inflicting on the group conditions of life calculated to bring about its physical destruction in whole or in part

Boko Haram does this when it attacks Christian communities and churches. It also does so in its caliphate, where Christians are subjugated, taxed, tortured, and discriminated against. In addition, forced conversions and forced marriages work toward eradicating Christians from Nigeria. Forced conversions turn Christians to Muslims and forced marriages produce more Muslim children as children grow up in their father's religion. These conversions are being instigated through kidnappings, as well as through violent attacks.

Imposing measures intended to prevent births within the group
There does not seem to be any measures, at this time, that are specifically intended to prevent Christians from procreating. All measures, at this point in time, seem to be pointed at the killing and displacing of Christians.

Forcibly transferring children of the group to another group
Although many children are being transferred to other areas of the country for their safety, it is not apparent that this is the targeted outcome of the attacks by Boko Haram. The group is trying to exterminate Christians, not transfer them.

Conclusion
Boko Haram meets the requirement for genocide on 3 out of 5 points. It only takes one to qualify. In addition to the overwhelming evidence of killing, injuring, and displacing of Christians by Boko Haram, there are also statements from the leadership of Boko Haram about the desire to wipe out Christians. There is no doubt that Boko Haram is waging genocide against the Christians in Nigeria.

Discussion Questions
1) Do you think the army should have released the names of the 25 towns that Boko Haram is targeting? Why or why not?

2) Would you try to escape from the Islamic Caliphate?

3) What would you do if you were questioned about a friend that you had spoken to? Would you lie to Boko Haram? Would you tell everything? Or would you do something different?

4) Would you be angry toward the person that spoke about you with Boko Haram? Even if Boko Haram threatened them with their life? How would you react?

5) What does community mean to you? Is your community part of your identity?

6) Should the international community be doing anything? If so, what?

Bring Back Our Girls

The kidnapping that got the attention of the world. Most did not know of Boko Haram until this day. Terrorism experts and intelligence professionals had been honed in on Boko Haram, but it was not high on the priority lists for politicians as it was mainly a Nigerian issue. However, this issue brought Boko Haram worldwide notoriety. Had Islamic State not taken the spotlight, we would still be talking about Boko Haram.

Although the media followed this case, many did not report the Christian aspect to the incident. Chibok Local Government Area (LGA) is over 90% Christian and all but 15 of the girls kidnapped were Christian. It should be noted that Chibok LGA is in the Northern part of the country, in Borno state. The North of Nigeria is predominantly Muslim. Choosing Chibok was no accident. It was chosen because of its majority religion of Christianity. This is just further evidence that Christian girls are targeted in Boko Haram kidnappings.

Since the kidnapping, at least 11 parents have died. Seven fathers were killed in an attack on a nearby village. Four more parents died of heart failure, high blood pressure and other illnesses that the community blames on the trauma caused by the abduction.[136]

So what has happened to these girls? What are the facts?

Case

When: April 14, 2014
Perpetrator: Boko Haram
Victims: 276 Female students (some manage to escape)
Where: Government Girls Secondary School, Chibok Village, Borno State, Nigeria
Religion: 95% of the kidnapped girls were Christian

Timeline

April 14: Boko Haram kidnaps 276 girls from the Government Girls Secondary School in Chibok Village, Borno State, Nigeria.

April 16: Borno state government offers a $300,000 reward for information leading to the rescue of the kidnapped girls. The President, Goodluck Jonathan, holds a meeting to discuss ways forward. The Nigerian military issues a statement saying all the girls have been freed and only 8 are missing.

April 17: Military retracts its statement, admitting that the girls are still in the hands of Boko Haram. Parents of the missing girls go into the Sambisa forest, near Cameroon, to look for the girls. They return and claim that they saw no Nigerian soldiers in the forest.

April 18: Major General Chris Olukolade admitted their report was incorrect but it was not intended to deceive the public.

April 19: The headmistress of the school appeals to the Nigerian government to do more and to Boko Haram to have mercy. She also confirms that 52 girls have managed to escape.

April 22: The headmistress tells BBC that at least 190 girls are missing. Her statement contradicted a local state governor who claimed around 80 were missing.

April 24: Parents of the girls, with other concerned Nigerians, take to social media to get the attention of the world. Their aim is to put international pressure on the Nigerian government.

Ibrahim Abdullah (lawyer) sends the first tweet using #BringBackOurGirls.

April 30: Million Woman March – about 500 people, dressed in red, gathered to deliver a letter to the National Assembly complaining the government was not doing all it could.

May 1: Parents stage a protest calling on government to do more. These protests become daily.

May 2: President Goodluck Jonathan creates a fact-finding committee. US Secretary of State John Kerry announces that the US is prepared to do everything possible to help Nigeria. Nigerian police say Boko Haram is holding 223 girls, after 53 of the initial 276 escape.

May 4: President Goodluck Jonathan made his first public statement since the abduction. He sought assistance from the US and other world leaders.

May 5: Boko Haram releases a video statement. Abubakr Shekau acknowledges that Boko Haram is responsible and threatens to sell some of the girls. The White House confirms it is helping Nigeria. Rumors abound that the girls have been moved to other countries. The US says that it has information that the girls are in Chad and Cameroon but both countries deny the girls are on their soil.

May 6: President Obama says this event will help mobilize the international community against Boko Haram. He acknowledges that US experts are being dispatched to help locate girls. Eleven more girls are abducted in Borno State.

May 7: President of France offers Nigeria a "special team" to look for the girls. Britain offers a team of experts. China promises to make available any intelligence gathered by its satellites and intelligence services. The #BringBackOurGirls hashtag campaign hits 1 million tweets. The US First Lady Michelle Obama posts a picture of herself with the hashtag.

May 9: Experts from US and UK arrive in Nigeria. Amnesty International accuses Nigeria's military of ignoring warnings before the abduction. Their accusation is based on a credible source that told the organization that the army was notified four hours in advance. The government says it doubts the report but promises to investigate.

May 11: The governor of Borno State says he has information on the location of the girls and has passed the information to the military. He does not believe the girls are in Chad or Cameroon.

May 12: Boko Haram releases another video. The missing schoolgirls are in the video stating that they have converted to Islam. Boko Haram states that it will release the girls in exchange for all imprisoned militants.

May 17: Summit is held in Paris, France regarding Boko Haram. The UK offered military advisors but cautioned that Nigeria must take its security responsibility seriously.

May 21: Nigeria's ambassador to the United States responds to disparaging remarks by Senator John McCain. The ambassador assured the public that the government was doing all it could.

May 25: Nigerian authorities are said to have started, then called off, a deal of swapping Boko Haram prisoners for the girls.

May 27: The Nigerian military claims it knows where the girls are but will not use force to rescue them. It is believed that Nigeria's president received a video from Boko Haram. The video was of the girls pleading for the president to spare their lives by doing a prisoner swap. The government has neither confirmed nor denied this incident but does say that there was never a deal on the table.

May 30: A civilian militia found two of the kidnapped girls raped, "half-dead" and tied to a tree. The militia members claimed that four other girls had been killed.

June 2: Reports emerge regarding four girls that escaped. One girl detailed that Boko Haram had split the girls into three groups.

June 20: The committee submits its report, confirms the kidnap, and says that 219 girls are still in the hands of captors.

June 26: Levik, a Washington DC public relations firm, had received a contract worth more than $1.2 million from Nigeria to work on international and local media narratives surrounding the kidnapping.

June 27: UN Security Council blacklists Boko Haram terrorist group leader Abubakr Shekau.

July 1: A businessman suspected of carrying out the kidnappings was arrested.

July 12: Pakistani human rights activist, Malala Yousafzai, visits Nigeria and meets with five of the girls who escaped Boko Haram.

July 14: Malala visits the Nigerian president.

July 15: The meeting between President Goodluck Jonathan and the parents of the kidnapped girls falls through. It is reported the parents cancelled. The President blames the #BringBackOurGirls campaigners for delaying the parents.

July 16: Parents explain that they did not intentionally shun the meeting. They were unaware of the meeting until the day of, when they received the invitation.

July 22: The rescheduled meeting is held.

September 10: Goodluck Jonathan orders campaign posters to be brought down that used #BringBackGoodluck2015.

September 26: One girl is found severely traumatized. It is unclear if she escaped or was released by Boko Haram.

October 12: Reports emerged that four girls from the original kidnapped group had escaped. They claimed they had been held in Cameroon and raped everyday. They walked three weeks to get back to Nigeria.

October 17: Nigeria's chief of defense staff announced that Boko Haram had agreed to an immediate cease-fire and the release of the girls.

October 27: Report from Human Rights Watch detailing the abuses endured by women in Boko Haram camps.

November 1: Abubakr Shekau denied there was any cease-fire agreement.

November 14: Chibok is overrun by Boko Haram and is now part of the Islamic Caliphate.

November 15: Military claims it has retaken the town.

What Happened?

It was evening on April 14, 2014. Hundreds of girls were sleeping in the dorms at the school. They were there to take their exams before graduation. The school was being briefly opened up just for these tests, as the security situation had forced them closed.

They awoke to gunfire. As they looked, they saw men in camouflage approaching. Believing the military had arrived to save them from an attack, the girls let their guard down. "Don't worry. Nothing will happen to you," Sanya reported the man as saying. The girls calmed down, thinking they were in safe hands.

The men gathered up food and supplies then set the school on fire. Then they herded all the girls into trucks and on to motorcycles. Suddenly, the men were shooting their guns into the air and shouting "Allahu Akbar." The girls now realized that they were not safe. Many started praying.

The girls reached the Boko Haram camp around noon.

Since this incident, a little over 50 girls have escaped. Their tales are harrowing. Rumors run rampant. The government either lies continually or has no idea what it is doing. Families are protesting daily. Meanwhile, the town of Chibok has been taken over by Boko Haram.

And the world has forgotten.

What is Being Done?
The Nigerian government claims it knows where the girls are but will not go after them. They say they are concerned of collateral damage.

The international community seems to have given up, despite its earlier rally calls. Many countries pulled their advisors out.

Advocacy groups and religious organizations are trying to lend aid. Social media campaigns and petitions continue.

Governments have sent money to help the girls who have escaped. It is unclear if the money is being used properly.

Christian communities within Nigeria are attempting to make one of the issues for the upcoming election about the reunification of the kidnapped girls with their families.

What is Boko Haram Doing with These Girls?

Unfortunately, nothing good. Based on stories from those that escaped from this kidnapping, and other kidnappings, these girls are first given the choice to convert. Those that do not convert are subjected to indescribable treatment.

The girls are forced into marriage. Many are raped continually. They are forced into servant hood (cleaning, cooking, washing, etc.). Some are chosen to help carry loot back to camp after a raid. Others are taken to battle and are forced to carry bullets and weaponry. On occasion, some have been forced to kill men, or lure men into ambushes.

They are continually abused on an emotional and spiritual level, in addition to the physical abuse.

Some speculate that they may be used as suicide bombers. This has yet to be corroborated.

All in all, it is unclear what has been done with the Chibok girls. Threats to sell them and/or marry them off have been made. Based on the history of this group, and the witness accounts of previous abductees, it can be assumed that the current situation of these girls is anything but good.

Discussion Questions

1) Would you continue to send your child to school if you lived in this area?

2) Do you think the government is right in its decision to not go rescue the girls because some might be killed?

3) Would you enact your own vigilante justice, knowing you might be killed in the process and your child not released?

What is Being Done?

It is important to get the big picture of what is being done in Nigeria. However, this section is by no means exhaustive as it is not the focal point of the report. This short overview of what is being done will show you just how confusing things are, making aid to the victims hard to organize and implement.

Medical – Related to Violence

Many of the victims and their family members expressed the ongoing anguish resulting from their ordeal, including deep fears of re-abduction, sleeplessness, and frustration for insufficient support from the government. However, of the victims interviewed, only the Chibok students who escaped from Boko Haram captivity had received any counseling and medical care, and the care received was quite limited. None of the other victims of abduction or other violations, all from desperately poor families, had received or were aware of any government supported mental health or medical care. The federal and state funds, set up with support from international agencies and foreign governments in the wake of the high-profile Chibok abductions, have targeted the escaped Chibok girls but appear not to have widely benefitted the many other victims of Boko Haram abuses.[137]

Missionaries, Ministries and NGOs

There are missionaries in Nigeria. However, due to security concerns, it is very hard to find accurate information on them. Much of what is publicly known comes through mentions in news articles.

An unnamed Nigerian Christian missionary couple resident near Chibok, Borno State, had rallied round to find the pupils some private donors who mobilised funds and offered them scholarship for a two-year high school studies in the US.[138]

Here is a list of organizations known to have missionaries or operations in Nigeria. The missionary names and locations are not listed in an effort to protect them.

- Christian Aid Mission
- Christian Reformed World Missions – focuses on Christian Education, Evangelism & Discipleship, and Leadership Development
- Voice of the Martyrs
- Stefanos Foundation
- Release International
- Catholic Relief Services
- Christian Association of Nigerian-Americans
- Pentecostal Fellowship of Nigeria

Here is a list of NGOs that are known to be helping victims in Nigeria.

- Educate After Escape
- United Nations High Commissioner for Refugees (UNHCR) is helping the refugee crisis both in and outside of Nigeria
- Red Cross
- Doctors Without Borders

Governments

European Union

The EU is providing emergency funds for the internally displaced within Nigeria. An estimated 5 million Euros will be allocated.[139]

France

Although not helping Nigeria directly, France is in the fight against Boko Haram in its former colonies: Chad, Cameroon, Niger and Mali. They are facilitating greater intelligence coordination and analysis on transnational militant movements.[140]

Israel

Israel attempted to sell an American-made Cobra helicopter to Nigeria. However, the US blocked the sale.

United Kingdom

The United Kingdom is active in its support to Nigeria in terms of security, according to its website, however it is unclear how much aid has been received and/or accepted by the Nigerian government.

United States

The US$100 million program aims to pilot 500 safe schools in northern Nigeria with a focus on school and community-level interventions. The program intends to organize community security groups consisting of teachers, parents, police, community leaders and more robust physical security in schools, including armed guards and a rapid response system, as well as counselors to work with students who are at risk of attack. The program is projected to help some of the 10.5 million children who are out of school in Nigeria feel safe enough to return to their education.[141]

The US has helped Nigeria strengthen its security systems in its international airports. Nigeria now uses full body scanners. In addition Nigeria is a participant in the State Department's Trans Sahara Counterterrorism Partnership (TSCTP), an interagency effort that strives to increase regional counter-terrorism capabilities and coordination.[142]

The US gives $600 million a year to Nigeria for many different services, none of which are security related. In 2013, the US State Department requested $1 million in Foreign Military Financing and another $1 million for military education and training. In addition the California National Guard also performs security cooperation activities with Nigeria. US support for Nigerian law enforcement is limited due to concerns of human rights abuses.[143]

US Aid is on the ground helping Nigeria's political system. They are helping to ensure fair elections and proper representation with the hope that this will help with the unrest in the country.

The Pentagon gave Nigeria Toyota trucks, communications equipment and body armor. However, Nigeria's officials accuse the US of failing to provide lethal weaponry that is needed to defeat Boko Haram.[144]

Support and help for Nigeria is waning significantly as relations between the two countries are strained. Nigeria accused the US of failing to help fight Boko Haram and the US condemned Nigeria for its dismal human rights record (the US has legal prohibitions against close dealings with militaries that have human rights abuses). In addition, Nigeria feels slighted that it is not receiving raw intelligence from US intelligence personnel but the US feels the government is too corrupted with Boko Haram supporters to share the information. When actionable intelligence was received by Nigeria, the country failed to act on it. Johnnie Carson, the State Department's former top diplomat for Africa, said in an interview,

> "Tensions in the U.S.-Nigeria relationship are probably at their highest level in the past decade. There is a high degree of frustration on both sides. But this frustration should not be allowed to spin out of control." [145]

Nigeria

The Nigerian government has a hard task. In addition to the terrorism inflicted by Boko Haram and the Fulani, there's a weak economy, political violence, struggles over oil, piracy, illicit trafficking, corruption, and more. In addition, there are accusations of extremists within the government's ranks, making any effective action almost impossible.

> *"The government is doing something, but the problem is beyond its ability. Even moderate Muslims fear for their lives. One Islamic scholar and two imams have been killed. But Nigeria's population is 178 million. President Goodluck Jonathan said Boko Haram has infiltrated government security. When government tries to do something, the infiltrators sabotage it. Even some top military generals have sympathies with Boko Haram. How can we deal with this if we cannot identify the enemy?"[146]*

Many in Nigeria feel that the government is not stepping up to the task. This may actually be the case.

However, despite the fact that the government has its work cut out for it, the responsibility to ensure its citizens are safe is still a primary one.

For unknown reasons, the Nigerian government cancelled the trainings that its military would have with US military.[147] These trainings were to train Nigeria's military on how to fight Boko Haram; something they desperately need.

A fund was set up to support victims, the Victim's Support Fund. However, many are questioning the government about the program. They note that the money was not being used to help Internally Displaced Persons or other victims of Boko Haram.[148]

There are accusations by the families of the kidnapped Chibok girls that the government is trying to silence them. The accusations range from blocking protests to preventing air travel.[149]

Nigerian Military

It is hard to lay criticism at the feet of the military, yet it must be done. According to almost all reporting, there is no cohesive leadership directing the operations of the military. Many times the military just doesn't show up, or doesn't show up on time. Even more frightening, are reports of the military abandoning their posts, running away, and leaving their weaponry behind.

> *As Boko Haram blocked exit roads from Gwoza and went door-to-door killing people, Nigerian military officials abandoned their weapons and fled, leaving Boko Haram unchallenged. "Now these weapons have fallen into the hands of Boko Haram. A few people were able to escape to the mountainside, just exactly like is happening in northern Iraq. A few people are holding out on the mountains, but most of the people in the village are being slaughtered. There is no communication between Gwoza and other parts of the country."* Ojutiku, to the Baptist Press.

United States Africa Command assesses the military of being extremely corrupt, poorly equipped, and "in tatters."

> *"Ounce for ounce, Boko Haram is equal to if not better than the Nigerian military."*[150]

However, there are also reports of military successes. The military has captured and/or killed Boko Haram members. They have recaptured towns and villages that Boko Haram took over. They are engaged in the fight. But they fight a big enemy. An enemy that outguns them, bribes their leaders, obtains intelligence that the military doesn't even get, and doesn't abide by the rules of engagement. It is no wonder soldiers flee.

> *Sarah Sewall, the undersecretary of state for civilian security, democracy and human rights, said at a separate hearing that despite Nigeria's $5.8 billion security budget for 2014, "corruption prevents supplies as basic as bullets and transport vehicles from reaching the front lines of the struggle against Boko Haram."*[151]

In addition, the families of the military personnel are also tired of burying their dead. They feel that their husbands and sons are being sent out to be slaughtered. Without proper equipment, and with corruption abounding, they don't want their service members fighting. There is no fighting chance.

This view is so prevalent that the families are staging protests. One such protest, estimated at 300 women and 500 children, lasted two days at a military base in Maiduguri.

> *"No weapons for our husbands, no trip to Gwoza or any volatile place. We are tired of burying our loved ones"* Thabita John, to the Baptist Press.

> *"I was told that many Nigerian soldiers refused to go and confront Boko Haram because their wives protested. They felt they were just sending their husbands to an untimely death. "* Ojutiku, to the Baptist Press.

Aside from their families not supporting the effort, they themselves have incredibly low morale. Government forces complain of being outnumbered and outgunned by Boko Haram. They say the have no leadership, not enough food on the battlefield, and little, if any, compensation for their work. [152] To top it off, they are being accused of killing civilians and burning down their homes. Human rights organizations accuse the military of violence against citizens. Often, the government troops respond to a Boko Haram crisis with such brute force that many civilians are killed. The government has not properly investigated the veracity of these claims, ergo the trust of the Nigerian people in their military has been eroded.

Military members also feel like they are being attacked on all sides. Boko Haram is attacking Nigeria, the citizenry of Nigeria does not trust them, the government does not provide adequate resources or pay, their families are in angst over everything, and now, those that decide to mutiny are brought up on charges and sentenced to execution by firing squad. The military is truly in a no win situation with no silver lining to be seen.

It is hard to determine how much blame should be left at the feet of the military. Truly, everyone wants the military to fight. That is what it is there for. On the other hand, it is hard to blame someone for refusing to fight when they are not being fed, not getting paid (which means their families are not getting fed), and aren't being given the weaponry that will enable them to win the battle.

There is absolutely no excuse for anyone to be killing civilians and burning down their houses. Those people should be prosecuted just as any other criminal would be. These people should be held accountable in order to obtain justice and in order to restore faith in the military.

The military, as a whole, has a tough situation to face. Without proper leadership, and without proper resources, they truly are heading into a battle they will be lucky to escape from.

How You Can Help

Do you want to help out the Nigerian Christians? Here is a list of organizations known to be reputable that are helping out on the ground in Nigeria. Hopefully, this list will grow.

- Serving in Mission
- Voice of the Martyrs
- Christian Aid Mission

There are also organizations that advocate on behalf of Nigeria and/or its citizens. Here is a list of these organizations. Many have petitions you can sign.
- Amnesty International
- #BringBackOurGirls and #BBOG hashtag campaigns on social media are still ongoing.
- International Christian Concern

Do you know someone, or have connections to an organization, that works in Nigeria? If you do, please connect them with me (see About the Author section for contact info). Be a part of advocating for those being massacred in Nigeria.

Discussion Questions

1) Do you think the international community is doing enough? Why or why not?

2) How do you feel about the actions of the military? Do you blame them for abandoning their posts?

3) What do you think needs to be done to help Nigeria?

Is It Worth It?

As you read through this book, you may have had many questions about persecuted Christians. You may ask, "Why don't these people move? Why don't they fight back? Why don't they convert? Is the cause really worth the cost?" These questions are completely valid, but the answers are somewhat complicated.

Some do fight back. Some move. But the majority doesn't. I will try to answer these questions to the best of my ability. The answers fall to one entity: Jesus, the Messiah.

To fully understand the Christian and why the individual acts the way they do, one must understand what Christians believe. It is important to understand that in all religions, Christianity included, there are many who claim to be believers, but in their hearts are not.

What Do Christians Believe?

At the beginning of time, when God created the world and humans, Adam and Eve, the first humans, disobeyed God by eating the fruit of the one tree that God forbade them to eat. This disobedience was the first sin. The couple chose to follow Satan rather than God. Because of this, God cast the couple out of the Garden of Eden and punished them. Women would have pain in childbirth, humans would be born with sin in their hearts, men would always toil, *et al.* This one act caused humanity to be separated from God.

For all have sinned and come short of the glory of God. Romans 3:23

Because humans were separated from God, they had laws to follow and sacrifices to perform in order to bring themselves in God's favor.

> **Definition of Sin**
> There is just one thing that separates a person from God. That one thing is sin.
>
> The Bible describes sin in many ways. Most simply, sin is our failure to measure up to God's holiness and His righteous standards. We sin by things we do, choices we make, attitudes we show, and thoughts we entertain. We also sin when we fail to do right things. The Bible affirms our own experience – "there is none righteous, not even one." No matter how good we try to be, none of us does right things all the time.
>
> God says that every person who has ever lived is a sinner, and that any sin separates us from God. We are all sinners.

After the establishment of Israel in Biblical times, Jesus the Messiah came to earth. He was a willing sacrifice (crucifixion) in order to save human kind. He was the last sacrifice needed to absolve the sin of humanity. Now, in order for humans to be able to live in God's graces, they did not need to sacrifice animals. They needed to believe in and love Jesus, and then live for Him.

God demonstrates His own love for us in this: While we were still sinners, Christ died for us. Romans 5:8

He saved us, not because of righteous things we had done, but because of His mercy. Titus 3:5

For it is by grace you have been saved, through faith - and this not from yourselves, it is the gift of God - not by works, so that no one can boast. Ephesians 2:8-9

If you confess with your mouth, "Jesus is Lord," and believe in your heart that God raised him from the dead, you will be saved.

For it is with your heart that you believe and are justified, and it is with your mouth that you confess and are saved. Romans 10:9-10

Because of Jesus' resurrection, defeating death, Christians' belief in Jesus means that on Judgment Day, their souls will be covered in Jesus' (the final sacrifice's) blood, absolving them of their punishment (death and hell). The true believers will be heirs of the Kingdom of Heaven.

For the wages of sin is death, but the gift of God is eternal life in Jesus Christ our Lord. Romans 6:23

For God so loved the world that He gave his one and only Son, that whoever believes in him shall not perish, but have eternal life. John 3:16

"Truly, truly, I say to you, he who hears My word, and believes Him who sent Me has eternal life. He does not come into judgment, but has passed from death to life." John 5:24

> **Definition of Trinity**
> The doctrine of the Trinity is not polytheism. Christianity does not believe in three gods. The belief is that there is one God, and three divine entities. Thus Jesus the Son is God, God the Father is God, and the Holy Spirit is God, yet all three are distinct from each other.
>
> It can be described as 1x1x1=1. (Jesus) x (Father) x (Holy Spirit) = (God). Each divine entity is its own, yet they are the same. Each 1 in the equation is its own entity, separate from the others. Yet each 1 is the same as the other 1s. And all equal 1.

After Jesus was resurrected, He came back to earth for 40 days. When He left (transfiguration), He sent the Helper (Holy Spirit). The Holy Spirit is the actual presence of God, active and alive, within Christians. The Holy Spirit is what prompts a person to believe and follow Jesus. Once the person does, the Holy Spirit draws the

Christian near to God, indwelling in the person and giving birth to a new spirit (being born again).

"But the Helper, the Holy Spirit, whom the Father will send in my name, he will teach you all things and bring to your remembrance all that I have said to you." John 14:26

(Jesus to the Disciples) *"I still have many things to say to you, but you cannot bear them now. When the Spirit of truth comes, He will guide you into all the truth for He will not speak on His own authority, but whatever He hears He will speak, and He will declare to you the things that are to come. He will glorify me, for He will take what is mine and declare it to you. All that the Father has is mine; therefore I said that He will take what is mine and declare it to you."* John 16:12-15

And Peter said to them, "Repent and be baptized every one of you in the name of Jesus Christ for the forgiveness of your sins, and you will receive the gift of the Holy Spirit." Acts 2:38

"Flesh gives birth to flesh, but the Spirit gives birth to spirit. You should not be surprised at my saying, 'You must be born again.' The wind blows wherever it pleases. You hear its sound, but you cannot tell where it comes from or where it is going. So it is with everyone born of the Spirit." John 3:6-8

With the understanding of the core beliefs of Christians, understanding their reasoning will be a little easier. Keep in mind that the non-Christian view of "reasoning" is quite different than a Christian's. A Christian strives to follow the reasoning of God, something that is often illusive to humans and may seem counter-intuitive.

It needs to be noted that Christians, in the midst of their persecution, may or may not be consciously thinking about the concepts we are about to discuss. Sometimes, possibly in a jail cell or some other instance of long suffering, the Holy Spirit will lead the Christian to think upon these truths and then proceed to act them out. Other times, the Christian acts instinctively based upon the knowledge and experience they've received in their relationship with the Holy Spirit

It is important to remember that when a person believes in Christ, believes in their heart that God raised Him from the dead, they are saved. Upon being truly saved (not just being born into a Christian family, but consciously choosing to follow Jesus), the person is filled with the Holy Spirit. God is literally living inside the person. This changes the character of the Christian. Because of this change, there are times when the person is acting in the will of God without thinking about it. The Christian, through the Holy Spirit, knows what it is God wants them to do, and they just do it. They can't help it. They want so badly to please God, that they do it, even when it doesn't make sense. Later on, if they are still living, they may ponder on the theology behind their actions. But in the midst of the incident, the Christian just wants to please God.

The true Christian knows that there is nothing that they can do to be worthy. They know that Jesus paid the ultimate price, as a sacrifice, to allow them the opportunity to be saved from eternal damnation. Therefore, they live their life working to please God, no matter the price.

Why Do Christians Allow Themselves to be Killed?

In this section, you will begin to understand why Christians allow atrocities to be committed against them. For the Christian, their life is not their own. It is God's. God owns the Christian's physical life and their eternal soul.

As you read, you will periodically see references to Muslim beliefs contrasted with Christianity's beliefs. These references juxtapose the extremist Islamic beliefs of Boko Haram and the Fulani with Christianity.

Persecution is Not a Surprise

Persecution looks different in various places around the world. It can be as obvious as beheading someone for their belief in Jesus and as hidden as a manager preventing a Christian from being promoted because the Christian's holy lifestyle makes the manager uncomfortable.

Christians are not surprised when persecution comes. It is expected. Jesus told His people that suffering and persecution would come to them.

"If the world hates you, know that it has hated me before it hated you. If you were of the world, the world would love you as its own; but because you are not of the world, but I chose you out of the world, therefore the world hates you. Remember the word that I said to you: 'A servant is not greater than his master.' If they persecuted me, they will also persecute you." John 15:18-20

The Christian knows that persecution is coming; it is not unexpected. The Christian also knows that their body will die. It is inevitable. However, for some, this inevitability is brought about through persecution. And that is ok. Because those that are persecuted are considered blessed in Christianity. It is an honor to follow in the footsteps of Jesus.

Pray For and Love Your Enemy?

Christians are not taught through Scripture to kill those that persecute them. They are not told to declare war on them or to in any way retaliate. Though the persecution comes, the Christian is to continue loving and praying. Jesus commanded that Christians pray for their enemies. Jesus desires that all would come to Him and be forgiven. Paul, formerly Saul, was a persecutor of Christians. Yet he was forgiven by Jesus and became one of the greatest evangelists. (Acts 9)

"You have heard that it was said, 'You shall love your neighbor and hate your enemy.' But I say to you, Love your enemies and pray for those who persecute you, so that you may be sons of your Father who is in Heaven. For He makes His sun rise on the evil and on the good, and sends rain on the just and on the unjust. For if you love those who love you, what reward do you have? Do not even the tax collectors do the same? And if you greet only your brothers, what more are you doing than others? Do not even the Gentiles do the same?" Matthew 5:43-47

Bless those who persecute you; bless and do not curse them. Romans 12:14

For the Christian, there is only the lost and the saved (unbelievers and believers). Because Jesus wants all people to be reconciled to Him, it is important to pray for persecutors to be saved. By showing love to the persecutors, some will come to Jesus. This is not possible on the strength of the Christian. The Holy Spirit is the driving force.

Who could love and pray for those that have raped your daughters, beheaded your husband, burnt down your village, and forced you to live in a cave?

A person who has the love of God living in them (the Holy Spirit). God loves. He is love. He requires His followers to have His kind of love. The Holy Spirit lives within a person and changes their spirit. Because of this, the Christian, although they are in immense pain and suffering, is able to see the condition of their persecutor's soul. The Christian can see that their persecutor needs the love of Jesus too - that only that love will change the persecutor's life and soul. Because the Christian has that love in them, God's love, they are able to pray and love everyone, even if they do not *like* everyone.

Paul, previously Saul, is a prime example of this. Saul was a persecutor of Christians. He describes himself as the chief of sinners, a blasphemer, persecutor, and insolent opponent. He came to faith in Jesus Christ (Acts 9). However, Paul did not stop there. He prayed, loved, and witnessed to everyone; even those that were persecuting him. Paul went to prison many times and was eventually killed for his unwavering belief and his unwillingness to stop sharing about Jesus' love.[153]

> About midnight Paul and Silas were praying and singing hymns to God, and the prisoners were listening to them, and suddenly there was a great earthquake, so that the foundations of the prison were shaken. And immediately all the doors were opened, and everyone's bonds were unfastened. When the jailer woke and saw that the prison doors were open, he drew his sword and was about to kill himself, supposing that the prisoners had escaped. But Paul cried with a loud voice, "Do not harm yourself, for we are all here." And the jailer called for lights and rushed in, and trembling with fear he fell down before Paul and Silas. Then he brought them out and said, "Sirs, what must I do to be saved?" And they said, "Believe in the Lord Jesus, and you will be saved, you and your household."

(Paul writing to Timothy) *I thank him who has given me strength, Christ Jesus our Lord, because he judged me faithful, appointing me to his service, though formerly I was a blasphemer, persecutor, and insolent opponent. But I received mercy because I had acted ignorantly in unbelief, and the grace of our Lord overflowed for me with the faith and love that are in Christ Jesus. The saying is trustworthy and deserving of full acceptance, that Christ Jesus came into the world to save sinners, of whom I am the foremost. But I received mercy for this reason, that in me, as the foremost, Jesus Christ might display his perfect patience as an example to those who were to believe in him for eternal life. 1 Timothy 1:12-16*

This type of behavior, to pray and love for those who persecute, was not just commanded, but it has been enacted since the beginning of Christianity. Yes, it is illogical to those who do not believe, but the ways of Jesus are not always logical to humans. Jesus' logic is perfect while human logic is not.

What kind of god would want his followers to suffer and not fight back? How is that love for the believer?

To fight back in the flesh does not ultimately fix the problem. The fight is between spiritual forces: those of Satan and those of God. To overcome evil, the spirit of evil must be overcome.

Do not be overcome by evil, but overcome evil with good. Romans 12:21

For we do not wrestle against flesh and blood, but against the rulers, against the authorities, against the cosmic powers over this present darkness, against the spiritual forces of evil in the Heavenly places. Ephesians 6:12

For the weapons of our warfare are not of the flesh but have divine power to destroy strongholds. 2 Corinthians 10:4

God the Father will indeed punish those that do not follow Him. The entire book of Revelation demonstrates God's wrath during the End Times. For those that die before that time, they will also receive extreme punishment through being thrust into hell, a place of eternal suffering, apart from God and anything good. What God is asking of the Christian is to leave judgment to Him. It is not the place of an imperfect being to lay judgment on another imperfect being. However, the One who is holy and just will lay down judgment when the timing is right. Then, He will not only judge unbelievers, but also Satan himself. Until that time, Christians are to fervently strive to bring more and more people to Jesus Christ in order to save as many people as possible from God's final judgment and wrath. Jesus commands them to do this through love, not violence. This concept is not unbeknownst to the secular world. Throughout history, major changes in social policy have occurred because of peaceful, non-violent movements. Martin Luther King, Jr. changed the American government, American laws, American enforcement, and American opportunities to provide equal treatment for black citizens. Mahatma Ghandi was able to help India gain its independence from Britain and inspired civil rights movements around the world. These are just two of many.

Many of those who sleep in the dust of the ground will awake, these to everlasting life, but the others to disgrace and everlasting contempt. Daniel 12:2

And the devil who had deceived them was thrown into the lake of fire and sulfur where the beast and the false prophet were, and they will be tormented day and night forever and ever. Revelation 20:10

They will make war on the Lamb, and the Lamb will conquer them, for he is Lord of lords and King of kings, and those with him are called and chosen and faithful. Revelation 17:14

And they have conquered him by the blood of the Lamb and by the word of their testimony, for they loved not their lives even unto death. Revelation 12:11

It is also worthy to note that God is not asking His followers to do anything that He, Himself, has not done. As Jesus was dying on the cross, having been beaten, flogged, ridiculed, tortured, stabbed and nailed to a cross, He asked for God the Father to forgive those that were persecuting, and killing, Him.

And Jesus said, "Father, forgive them, for they know not what they do." Luke 23:34

The Command to Live, Not Die

A nuance often lost in the talk about martyrdom. Many believe that anyone that dies because of their belief is a martyr. For this discussion, the definition for a Christian martyr held by the

Moody Bible Institute will be used. "Those who were killed because they refused to renounce their faith or because of active opposition to their witness for Christ."

> "O you who believe! Fight those of the disbelievers who are close to you, and let them find harshness in you, and know that Allah is with those who are the Al-Muttaqun (the pious).
> Quran 9:123."

The definition is important because it plays into motive. In the Islam of extremists, many aspire to be martyrs. In this religion, getting oneself killed makes one a martyr, as long as the intent was to further Islam. It is also important to note the above definition of martyrdom does not allow for malice. Someone dying with a malicious intent is not considered a martyr in the Christian faith.

In Christianity, persecution is expected. Because of this, it is natural to assume that many who are Christians will die because of the persecution. Many people are under the impression that if you are killed, and you are a Christian, you are a martyr. This is not the case. A Christian martyr is one that is killed because they do not renounce Jesus Christ. Christian martyrdom is predicated on a single, direct link to their witness: persecutor demands they renounce, the Christian says no, the Christian dies.

The second way to be a martyr is to die because of the Christian's witness for Christ. The person may not be asked to renounce Christ, but their testimony to/about Jesus causes them to be killed. This is an active (not passive) belief.

In no way is Christian martyrdom connected with purposefully getting oneself killed or murdering others to somehow justify the Christian martyrdom.

So why is all of this important? Because Christians are commanded to *live* for Christ. Yes, they may die, but their death is a result of their living. After all, God created humans to live, commanding them to be fruitful and multiply. He gave humans dominion over the animals and gave them every plant. The entire concept of dying was not originally in the plan for humans. Adam and Eve's sin (to follow Satan instead of God) lead to the punishment of experiencing death. This punishment affects all people and all generations. Jesus Christ is the Savior from this death. Jesus was the last sacrifice to cover humanity's sins and He conquered death, fully controlling it and using it to His desires. God sent Jesus to His disobedient creation to save them from the punishment they deserved. Although Christians will experience dying physically, they will never face the judgment of death. Again, God wants His followers to *LIVE*.

I appeal to you therefore, brothers, by the mercies of God, to present your bodies as a living sacrifice, holy and acceptable to God, which is your spiritual worship. Romans 12:1

For I know the plans I have for you, declares the Lord plans for welfare and not for evil, to give you a future and a hope. Jeremiah 29:11

The thief comes only to steal and kill and destroy. I come that they may have life and have it abundantly. John 10:10

May the God of hope fill you with all joy and peace in believing, so that by the power of the Holy Spirit you may abound in hope. Romans 15:13

For none of us lives to himself, and none of us dies to himself. For if we live, we live to the Lord, and if we die, we die to the Lord. So then, whether we live or whether we die, we are the Lord's. For to this end Christ died and lived again, that he might be Lord both of the dead and of the living. Romans 14:7-9

Whatever you do, work heartily, as for the Lord and not for men, Colossians 3:23

This concept, to live, is contrasted with Islam's desire to subjugate, kill, and be killed. As Boko Haram and the Fulani tribes attack and kill Christians in their efforts to follow their religion, Christians are striving to live life and to bring eternal life to other sinners. Christians are not looking to kill or to be killed. They are living their lives for Christ. That lifestyle may cause them to be killed. Islam encourages its followers to be killed (this is not considered suicide as the person is in battle and is not doing so out of despair). In this form of Islam, the goal is not to live. The goal is to die and receive the many rewards for doing so. The Islamic faith does not have a messiah that comes and saves them. Instead, a Muslim has to work to earn favor and eternity in paradise. They do this through jihad. In short, a Christian is rewarded for the way they *live;* a Muslim is rewarded for the way he *dies*.

Christians are NOT Afraid of Death

What? Who isn't afraid of death? To put it simply, Christians do not fear death. This is because Jesus has conquered death. Therefore, those that believe in Jesus Christ will not suffer death; they will enter the Kingdom of Heaven for eternity.

This is not to say that Christians do not fear *dying*. The act of dying can be painful. Who wants to experience pain? Jesus Himself did not want to experience the pain of torture and crucifixion. He did it because God the Father willed it in order to provide a path of salvation to those who yield to His call.

And going a little farther He fell on His face and prayed, saying, "My Father, if it be possible, let this cup pass from me; nevertheless, not as I will, but as you will." Matthew 26:39 ("this cup" refers to the arrest and crucifixion. Jesus knew it was imminent.)

However, once the body dies, the soul is released. A Christian's soul will go to eternal peace, Heaven. An unbeliever's soul will go to hell, a place of eternal torment. There are only two possibilities once the body dies; your soul goes to Heaven or your soul goes to hell. Your soul either belongs to Jesus or Satan. There is no in-between.

Death, for a Christian, is simply the act of leaving one's earthly body. Jesus has promised Christians new bodies in Heaven. Therefore, death is not to be feared for the Christian. It is the act of leaving the world and joining Jesus in Heaven, in a place with no suffering. For a Christian, Heaven is home, not the world. We were created to live in the Garden of Eden without pain or suffering. Because of our sin, we were thrust into a world controlled by the devil. Jesus, through His death and resurrection, created a way to overcome this world and go to Heaven, our home. Death is a part of life on the Christian's journey home.

Therefore we are always confident and know that as long as we are at home in the body we are away from the Lord. For we live by faith, not by sight. We are confident, I say, and would prefer to be away from the body and at home with the Lord. So we make it our goal to please him, whether we are at home in the body or away from it. 2 Corinthians 5:6-9

Why Do Christians Refuse to Deny Christ?

This is a very important question. It is especially important in context to Nigeria as Islam and Christianity differ starkly on this point.

A Christian will not deny Christ because of what Jesus has done for them. A Christian understands that Jesus was tortured and killed to pay the debt of his/her sin. Jesus, through His power, then conquered death and came back to life in order to give the Christian the gift of forgiveness. Because of this, the Christian will not suffer eternally, like the unbeliever. Jesus is so precious to the Christian that the Christian serves Jesus in every way. It is inconceivable to deny Him.

Consider this. You are thrown into a prison, where you are tortured night and day until you are almost dead, but not completely. Your torturers keep you alive just enough to feel every pain, but stop just short of killing you. They mentally and emotionally abuse you in addition to the physical abuse. You want to die, but they will not allow you to have that solace. Worst of all, you know you deserve it because of what you did.

Then, someone comes along, maybe a complete stranger, and tells the torturers that he/she will take your place. You are released. As you leave, struggling to see through your eyes, you see this stranger. That person is being led to your cell. You feel instant relief that it is not going to be happening to you anymore. Then some other emotion sets in. You realize that the person saving you is innocent. They had nothing to do with your guilt. They will be suffering inhumane torture because of you. You feel sick.

You've arrived home and you learn that the stranger has been freed. This stranger was able to defeat the torturers. You are elated. You learn all you can about this stranger. Upon finding their location, you immediately go to the stranger to give your thanks. The stranger tells you that they did it out of love. You know there is absolutely no way to pay this person back for what they've done. You see the scars from the abuse. You vow to yourself to do whatever this person needs done. You know that if they are in a fight, you will fight with that person. Even unto death.

This is the kind of loyalty that Christian believers have toward Jesus. They know that Jesus conquered hell and death so that believers would not have to suffer it. Jesus took all of the guilt and punishment in order to save the believer. Because of this, it is unfathomable to the Christian to deny Jesus in any capacity.

Jesus also warns that "whoever denies me before men, I also will deny before my Father who is in Heaven," (Matthew 10:33). Therefore, should a person deny Christ, the individual will not enter Heaven and will instead enter hell.   There is no waiver.

"Truly, I say to you, all sins will be forgiven the children of man, and whatever blasphemies they utter, but whoever blasphemes against the Holy Spirit never has forgiveness, but is guilty of eternal sin." Mark 3:28-29

Christians are also forbidden to lie. In Christianity, it is a sin to commit a lie. This includes lies of omission and being deceitful. There is no exception to this. Nowhere are Christians told that it is allowable to lie in certain circumstances.

The Lord detests lying lips, but He delights in people who are trustworthy. Proverbs 12:22

This is in stark contrast to Islam. Islam allows for lying in order to hide ones faith from others. It also allows for lying when it serves a greater purpose. It is intertwined into the Islamic faith in many ways. Lying is not tied to morals. It is a method to ensure that honor is upheld. It is also a means to an end. If lying achieves the end goal, then it is allowable. Islam goes even further to differentiate between the permissible and impermissible lies.

Any one who, after accepting faith in Allah, utters Unbelief,- except under compulsion, his heart remaining firm in Faith - but such as open their breast to Unbelief, on them is Wrath from Allah, and theirs will be a dreadful Penalty. Qur'an 16:106

When it is possible to achieve such an aim by lying but not by telling the truth, it is permissible to lie if attaining the goal is permissible.[154]

A Muslim who is subject to severe religious persecution—which exposes him to a reasonable fear of death or severe bodily injury unless he renounce Islam—is permitted, but not required, to renounce Islam verbally even though he remains inwardly a faithful Muslim.

Taqiyya is of fundamental importance in Islam. Practically every Islamic sect agrees to it and practices it ... We can go so far as to say that the practice of taqiyya is mainstream in Islam, and that those few sects not practicing it diverge from the mainstream ... Taqiyya is very prevalent in Islamic politics, especially in the modern era.[155]

> **Taqiyya** – an individual can deny his faith or commit illegal/blasphemous acts while at risk of persecution
>
> **Tawriya** – in English, this concept is similar to double entendre. The actual words of the statement are true, however there is another meaning. Example: Someone asks if you can lend him or her your car. Your response is that you don't have an extra car. (but you DO have an extra SUV)

Allah (Muslim god's name) uses deceit, unlike Yahweh (Christian God's name). If Allah is deceitful, then it can stand to reason that his followers are allowed to be deceitful as well. Thus, Islam allows for denial of Allah.

And they (the disbelievers) schemed, and Allah schemed (against them): and Allah is the best of schemers. Qur'an 3:54 (the Arabic word "makara" used for "scheme" literally means "deceit")

The Islamic prophet also allows for lying in three different scenarios: to reconcile quarrels, to one's wife, or jihad.

That she heard Allah's apostle saying, "He who makes peace between the people by inventing food information or saying good things, is not a liar." Bukhari Vol 3:857

Especially in the jihadists' and extremists' views of Islam, lying and deception are permissible. An Arabic legal manual devoted to jihad describes deception as a way of war and is permissible in any instance that involves duping one's enemy. [156] Therefore, denying one's faith in Allah is permissible as long as it is serving to destroy one's enemy and further Islam. This is very much in line with the rationalization that committing suicide in order to kill non-Muslims is not actually suicide because it is part of the war against infidels. Thus, the suicide is actually a weapon of war, thus the person killed is not subjugated to the laws concerning suicide.

Conclusion

Christians strongly desire to live because Jesus commanded it. It is through life, and even death, that Jesus's Holy Spirit reaches others and brings them to saving faith. Every Christian was a non-believer upon birth. At some point in their life, they heard God calling them to believe in Jesus. This calling came with the understanding of what Jesus had done for them. This knowledge, and understanding, compels the Christian to follow Jesus. Hence why believers don't deny Christ.

Though both Christians and Muslims are not afraid of death, the predicate is different. Christians believe that Jesus owns their earthly body as well as their soul. Therefore they take solace in their calling to be persecuted. Jesus told them the persecution would come. It is no surprise. Because their body is not their own, Christians understand that it can be taken away. It is God's creation to do what He pleases. Although death may be painful, it is an obstacle that must be crossed in order to join Jesus in Heaven. Death is just a stepping-stone on their journey.

Discussion Questions

1) How do you feel about martyrdom? Does it make you uncomfortable?

2) Would you be able to stay firm in your faith at the cost of your life? Or at the cost of someone else's life?

3) Paul was used numerous times in the book as an example of martyrdom and living out your life for Jesus. Who are some other people (in and out of the Bible) that you think are good examples? Why?

4) Christianity and Islam both have accepting views of martyrdom (although their views of martyrdom are entirely different). Are there other religions that are accepting of martyrdom? If so, explain.

5) Do you think it is ok to deny your faith? Define loyalty in your own words.

6) Do you think it is ok to lie? What circumstances, if any, do you think it is permissible to lie?

In Memory Of

Here is a list of the Christians killed in 2014 because of Nigeria's escalating violence by Boko Haram and the Fulani. This is in no way a full list. But to those that I could find, I wanted to give a place in my book. Some names may be repeats due to naming rituals creating multiple names for the same people and the same names for multiple people. I included all forms in case they were different people.

Christian Deaths by Boko Haram

Name	Age
Eluid Mshelizza Gwamma	44
Bulama Dajiba	
Bulama John	
Haruna Wadda	
Bitrus Kurma	
Haruna Kwatha	
Haruna Waruda	
Shaibu Galva	
Haruna Gwama	60
Joseph Yava	50
Markus Ngamtuka	58
Dabawa Ibrahim	16
Tsaudina Bulus	23
Shuwa Yakubu	15
Kewa Bitrus	47
Kulkwa Bitrus	8
Yakuba Godiya	65
Naomi John	50
Bitrus John	55
Son of Bitrus John	
Son of Bitrus John	
Jummai Sunday	63
Son of Jummai Sunday	
Sister of Jummai Sunday	
John	
Godiya John	
Aderenle Shinaba	12
Hannaniya Sini Kwajipwa	

Christian Deaths by Fulani

Name	Age
Agiya Maisamari	60
Talatu Agiya	26
Rhoda Agiya	35
Awolu Minday	3
Danbaba Agbun	75
Tasala Danbaba	45
Pheobe Danjuma	22
Maryamu Danjuma	19
Clement Danjuma	16
Hannatu	
Alheri Danbala	28
Lahleh Philip	20
Peace Phillip	3
Tina Audi	40
Larai Monday	30
Yanga Monday	35
Kulu Monday	18
Amina Sambo	45
Dan Peter	7
Ruth Peter	5
Hassana Peter	3
Zabi Felix	15
Amande Musa	80
Stephen Maichibi	55
Sarah Stephen	40
Paul Stephen	8
Japheth Ayuba	2
Rita Danjuma	3
Julius Jako	55
Rhoda Jako	45
Zok Alamba	22
James Dachung	45
Daniel Kahwong	68
Asabe Daniel Kahwong	45
Jennifer Daniel Kahwong	10
Rose Usaini	34
Simi Usaini	10
Precious Usaini	7
Baby Usaini	
Joel Ambo	
Yajuba Ambi	
Yamu Idzi	
Anche Ishaku	
Misalai Ngbo	
Ishaya Anche	
Monday Samson	

Name	Age
Husseina Jako	12
Gideon Mutang Kidum	
Ladi Mafulul	
Ladi Mafulul's 2 children	
Urawal (deaf woman)	
Likita Riku	
Likita Riku's wife	
Likita Riku's 3 children	
Isah Onum	60
Kahfa Timbong	
Tanden Nandang	
Takuba Changtim	
Andrew Bature	
David Gwong	22
Abin Kaawai	
Ruth Abin	
Indip	
Emma	
Cletus	
Bitrus	
Dauda	
Husband of Ema Okpanachi	
Husband of Abiye Edo	
Ezra Ibrahim	
Tina Aku	55
Kulu Danjuma	77
Mercy Silas	
Dr. Danjuma	37
Mother of Silas	
Daughter of Silas	
Jummai Likita Riku (pastor's wife)	
Child of Jummai Likita Riku	
Child of Jummai Likita Riku	
Child of Jummai Likita Riku	
Mother of Dang	
Wife of Dang	
Child of Dang	
Child of Dang	
Child of Dang	
Child of Dang	
Relative of Dang	
Relative of Dang	
Relative of Dang	
Jowl Anzah	
Jonathan Anche	
P-Square	

What is to Come in 2015?

Although no one can properly ascertain the future, a look at the trajectory of things can often lend a hand in preparing for what is to come.

I also want to let all of my readers know what they can expect to be added to the 2015 update on Nigeria's Christians. I hope to have an even more robust analysis based on wider-ranging data. I also hope to make connections with people on the ground.

Fulani

The issues between the Fulani and the mostly Christian farmers are long-standing and not likely to go away. Although these conflicts have been going on for quite some time, the level of violence and retaliation has increased significantly. Many speculate that the Fulani, at the very least, are being supplied with weaponry and resources. Don't expect this issue to fade. Sadly, I fully anticipate that attacks on Christians will become more frequent and more violent. It won't stop until Christians are completely eradicated from Nigeria.

> "The farmers and herdsmen have always fought. Why is it that only now they are using highly sophisticated weapons? Come on. They're getting sophisticates weapons and support form somewhere. They are attacking police, police stations, military barracks, government buildings, and innocent people. Clearly somebody is supporting them."[157]

This next year, I will continue to monitor the situation with the Fulani. Expect to see more robust numbers, to include tactics, number of Fulani injuries/deaths, deaths/injuries caused by the Fulani on non-Christians, and more. Although information is limited on these issues due to reporting, I continually work my contacts and network to create more contacts in order to get the most accurate information possible.

Boko Haram

This is definitely a problem that is not going away. Over the whole world, the jihadist cause has risen significantly and Boko Haram, alongside Islamic State, is leading the way. I fully expect this issue to increase significantly.

Without comprehensive strategies for attacking Boko Haram, and without international help for both the Nigerian government and the victims, this sad state of affairs will only grow exponentially. Unfortunately, both are not coming. The world does not see or hear the cries of the Nigerians. The issue is too far away.

More Christians will be displaced. More Christians will die or be injured. More Christians will have psychological and physical wounds that will not be attended to. More Christian abductions will occur.

But it won't just be Christians. Although Boko Haram is very focused on wiping out Christians, it also wants to wipe out anyone who disagrees with the group's activities. As Boko Haram's tactics have become more brutal, and as its attacks on Christians have risen dramatically, the group has also expanded its targets to include any that would oppose the group's advances.

We can also expect kidnappings to rise exponentially. Kidnapping reaps large rewards for Boko Haram and at very little, if any cost to the group. By kidnapping, the group achieves press coverage and ransom money. If they do not receive ransom money, they have women to use for sex, operational support, and for cooking & cleaning. Kidnapping also gives Boko Haram a propaganda edge that keeps the people of Nigeria in fear. Until there is a down side for Boko Haram, these kidnappings will not only continue, they will increase.

Next year, I will be very focused on producing numbers of all casualties on all sides of this issue: how many Christians, how many military, how many Boko Haram, how many Muslims, etc. Of course, tactics and motives will be analyzed. As I have engaged in research over the year, I have made many contacts. I will utilize all these contacts throughout the entire year to provide a more robust view of what is going on in Nigeria and I plan to provide more ways that you can get involved.

Other

What else could possibly be going on?! Well, there is plenty. It has come to my attention that al-Shabaab is broadening its influence and may be moving into Nigeria. In December 2014, there were attacks on Christians in Nigeria. I will take the time to sort through this to determine if this is a threat to Christians in Nigeria a few isolated incidents.

Boko Haram is moving into neighboring countries. Analysis is needed to see if the expanded violence will be Christian centered, or if Boko Haram is merely looking to seize more territory.

Piracy is another big issue. I do not believe this to be focused against Christians, but further research needs to be done to be certain. If pirates are targeting Christians, you will hear about it in the 2015 update to this book.

I would like to add a section from the Christians in Nigeria. Their words to you. I will try to make this happen. It is not easy. Reporters have a hard time even getting the information of each attack. Sometimes, they don't even know about an attack for weeks or months. I will work on it though and hopefully, we will be able to hear some encouraging stories from people on the ground.

Maps

States with Sharia Law in Nigeria
N
NIGER
CHAD
SOKOTO
KATSINA
JIGAWA
YOBE
BORNO
ZAMFARA
KANO
KEBBI
GOMBE
BENIN
KADUNA
BAUCHI
NIGER
CHAD
KWARA
ADAMAWA
PLATEAU
ABUJA
NASARAWA
OYO
TARABA
OSUN
11
KOGI
BENUE
OGUN
10
EDO
9
2
1
3
DELTA
5
4
12
7
6
8
CAMEROON
C.A.R.
Bight Of Benin
Gulf Of Guinea
Bight Of Biafra
1. EBONYI
2. ENUGU
3. ANAMBRA
4. ABIA
5. IMO
6. AKWA IBOM
7. RIVERS
8. BAYELSA
9. LAGOS
10. ONDO
11. EKITI
12. CROSS RIVER
0 100 200 Km
International Boundary
State Boundary
Sharia Law States
Copyright © 2015 Clay Murray, Jr

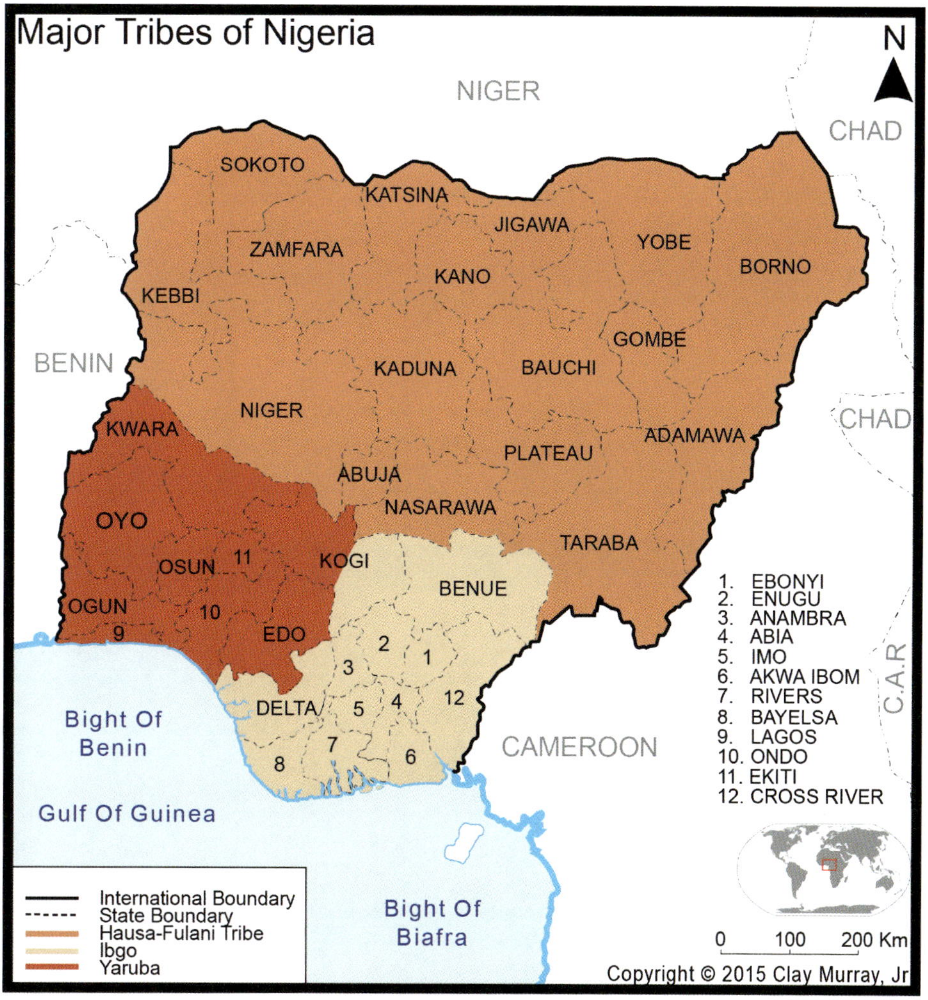

Major Tribes of Nigeria
N
NIGER
CHAD
SOKOTO
KATSINA
JIGAWA
YOBE
BORNO
ZAMFARA
KANO
KEBBI
GOMBE
BENIN
KADUNA
BAUCHI
NIGER
KWARA
ADAMAWA
CHAD
PLATEAU
ABUJA
NASARAWA
OYO
TARABA
OSUN
11
KOGI
BENUE
OGUN
10
9
EDO
2
1
3
DELTA
5
4
12
Bight Of Benin
7
6
8
CAMEROON
Gulf Of Guinea
C.A.R.
1. EBONYI
2. ENUGU
3. ANAMBRA
4. ABIA
5. IMO
6. AKWA IBOM
7. RIVERS
8. BAYELSA
9. LAGOS
10. ONDO
11. EKITI
12. CROSS RIVER
International Boundary
State Boundary
Hausa-Fulani Tribe
Ibgo
Yaruba
Bight Of Biafra
0 100 200 Km
Copyright © 2015 Clay Murray, Jr

Methodology

Research

In addition to monitoring the news, social media, humanitarian/religious organizations and think tanks, research was also conducted through peer reviewed articles, journals, organizations that monitor and analyze terrorism, and government reporting.

Effort was taken to read all sides of the issue (if more than one side exists) and to appropriately vet the information.

Biblical references have hyperlinks to Biblegateway.com. This website offers many translations and paraphrases of the Bible. For this book, only translations that are considered to be direct from the source are used. No paraphrasing is used, nor any translations from a translation.

Database

The database created through the researching of this book is available for others doing research and/or advocacy. Please go to www.LDMurray.com and submit an email request to discuss terms. The information will be provided in an editable Excel spreadsheet.

Google
Google alerts were set up for "Nigeria attacks," "Fulani" and "Boko Haram." These alerts were set up to deliver daily. This daily delivery provided all news results, across the globe, for those search terms. There were over 400 email alerts received, each with 1-39 results. This number is only in regard to the Google alerts; not news agencies, organizations, online reporting, etc.

The results were opened, a determination was made as to whether the content was relevant to Christian persecution, the relevant content was placed in a database for further analysis, and then filed into appropriate electronic files. While determining the veracity of the news sources, a determination was also made as to whether the incident was a repeat reporting incident. Care was taken to ensure that the data was not recorded twice.

Effort was made to differentiate between attacks perpetrated on Christians because of their faith and other attacks. Boko Haram, although it focuses on Christians, will sometimes target non-Christians (such as the military). Likewise, attacks perpetrated by the government and military are evaluated based on their motive; whether they attacked because of victim's religion or because of another reason. This book assumes that if the village/town is predominantly Christian, that the dead and injured are Christian. Efforts are made to parse out just the Christian numbers, but most reporting does not do so. It can be assumed that a small number of non-Christians are counted in these numbers, however, the numbers are not great.

Much effort was made to distinguish the motive behind the attacks as well as the profiles of the victims. Many times, the media will report an incident as religion-neutral when it is in fact not. Analysis was done on all reporting, pro-religion reporting, anti-religion reporting and religion-neutral reporting, to determine the religious aspects of each incident.

Left out of this book are numbers of Boko Haram members, military, police, Fulani, and all other non-Christian deaths and injuries. These numbers will hopefully be gathered and calculated in 2015's book in order to give a better perspective of what is going on in Nigeria.

Advocacy Groups and News Organizations

Email alerts, newsletter subscriptions, and social media were used to gather information from advocacy groups as well as Christian and humanitarian news organizations.

In addition to receiving the newsletters, a systematic search was also done on advocacy groups' websites, Facebook pages, and publications in order to glean additional information for this book. These searches were also used to verify numbers gleaned from Google searches. In addition, profiles of prisoners, martyrs, and others were gleaned from these advocacy groups.

Organizations that Provided Email Alerts

International Christian Concern
WORLD News Group
Pamela Gellar, Atlas Shrugs
Al- Monitor
Breaking Christian News
CBN News
Mission Network News
Agenzia Fides
Jihad Watch
Christians Headlines Daily
Christian Freedom International
Open Doors
Christianity Today
David Horowitz
Morning Star News
Gatestone Institute
Stratfor
American Center of Law and Justice
Worthy Brief
Voice of the Martyrs
Gospel for Asia
Christian Solidarity Worldwide
Release International
Human Rights Watch
Crisis Response International
Baptist Press

Council of Foreign Relations

Magazines and Paper Newsletters
Christianity Today
Persecution Magazine
WORLD magazine
TIME
International Christian Concern
Voice of the Martyrs

Social Media & Websites That Were Monitored
Facebook
Twitter
International Christian Concern
Voice of the Martyrs
Voice of the Martyrs Nigeria
Baptist Press
Morning Star News
Council of Foreign Relations
Jubilee Campaign
Barnabas Aid
Aid to the Church in Need
Human Rights Watch
United Nations
START Database
TRAC
Counter Extremism
Religion of Peace
Open Doors
Release International

Limitations

1) Many news organizations are not in English. The sole reliance on English versions may result in some information not being collected. It should be noted that because of this limitation, it is likely that there are more attacks on Christians than is reported in this book.

2) Most news outlets do not report the victims as Christian, even though they were targeted for their Christian belief. Because of this, the numbers produced in this report are likely lower than the actual count.

3) Although there are groups that advocate for persecuted Christians and groups that give aid to them, there is no comprehensive database to glean information from. This book is an attempt to create such a resource; a place to get historical facts, statistics on Christians, analysis, and more. However, because of the lack of focus from governments and the financial limitations these organizations face, there are likely attacks and persecution incidents that have gone un-reported. Thus, the numbers and situations provided in this book are likely less than what is actually occurring across the globe.

4) Due to the isolation of many villages in Nigeria, as well as the many conflicting agendas of the government, military, and civilian populations, news reporting can often be contradictory. Often, attackers will block routes out of the villages, preventing the villagers from acquiring help, which also delays reporting. In addition, the frequency of attacks in the same areas can often convolute the facts. Several incidents can be confused with one another or added together. Effort was taken to provide the most likely occurrence. Sources closest to the incident, as well as NGOs, were used when conflicts in reporting arose. When determining the number of injured and dead, the latest number was used as reporting can be very confused at the time of the attack. Time can also allow for organizations and news reporters to determine if the there were several attacks or just one, making the number of injured/dead different.

5) Due to vague reporting, the data regarding damages caused by attacks is significantly low. Many reports will use vague terms such as "many" when referring to the number of houses or churches burned. Also, because of the significant loss of life and trauma, people do not generally report damages. Their focus is on the ones they lost. Damages are extremely hard to quantify because of this. It can be assumed that the number of damages in this book is significantly lower than actuality.

###

Thank you so much for reading my book! I hope that it answered your questions and gave you a better understanding of Nigeria and its Christians. If you enjoyed it, please take a moment and leave me a review at your favorite retailer.

Thank you!

Laura Murray

Learn a little more about Laura and her book in her interview with Smashwords at https://www.smashwords.com/interview/ldmurray

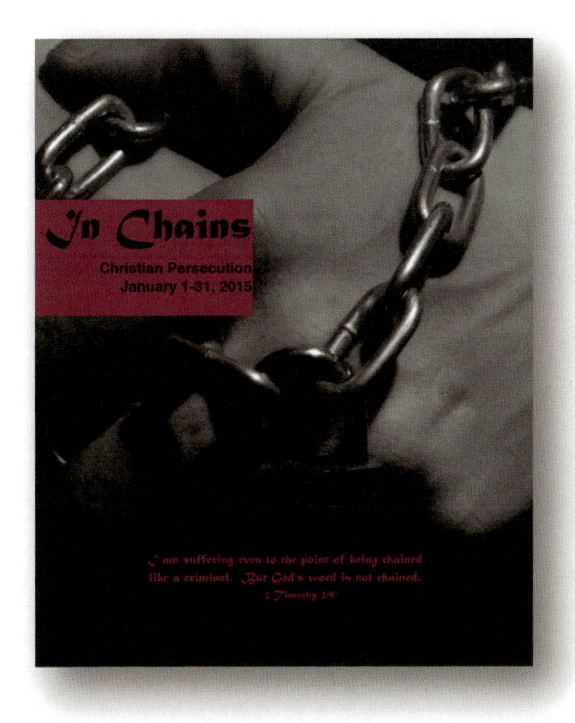

Sign up to receive "In Chains" monthly newsletter on Christian persecution around the world. It is FREE and you will receive top news stories, analysis, and statistics.
http://www.ldmurray.com/persecution.html

About the Author

Laura Murray is a writer and author. She currently writes freelance while authoring books. She received her Bachelor of Science in Political Science at the University of Louisville and her Masters of Strategic Intelligence at American Military University. She has worked with the Department of Homeland Security and the Kentucky State Police Intelligence Branch. Laura thoroughly enjoys writing papers and articles on security, intelligence, terrorism, and crime topics.

Laura left government work on the state and federal levels to work from home. Her new careers as a writer and author developed simultaneously. She currently writes articles on current issues, persecution, food, and raising children. She also contracts work with security companies, creating and writing reports. Of course, she also works on books and essays regarding Christian persecution around the world.

Laura strives to dig into what is really going on around the world and bring it to her readers in an understandable way. So many times, the media just doesn't connect the dots, or worse, they purposely hide the truth. Laura works to get to the bottom of these issues as much as possible. Her experience in government and her education gave her the skills she needs to do this effectively.

On her personal side, Laura is a homeschool mom, she loves to travel and cook, and she loves enjoying life.

Connect with Laura

Website: www.LDMurray.com
Facebook: www.Facebook.com/AuthorLauraMurray
Google+: https://plus.google.com/u/0/110088513889441387610/posts
Blog: http://followldm.blogspot.com/
Twitter: https://twitter.com/MurrayWonders
Smashwords: https://www.smashwords.com/profile/view/ldmurray

Acknowledgments

I want to take a moment to thank those who helped me in the creation of my first book.

CLAY MURRAY, JR
Thank you for editing, work with copyrights, and map analysis & creation.

PASTOR BILL PAGE
Thank you for the editing, advice, and guidance.

FAMILY & FRIENDS
I also want to say thank you to all of my family and friends who have been so supportive in this endeavor. I appreciate each and every one of you.

Image, Map, & Photo Credits

Cover Page Image
Image was purchased from Dmick27 at SelfPubBookCovers.com
SelfPubBookCovers.com/Dmick27

Introduction

Textbox 1
Created by Laura Murray with information and data gathered through her research and analysis. See Methodology Section for details on how information was gathered.

Nigeria

Information Table
Created by Laura Murray with information from: "Nigeria," *World Factbook: 2013-14*, U.S. Central Intelligence Agency Office of Public Affairs, accessed December 26, 2014, https://www.cia.gov/library/publications/the-world-factbook/geos/ni.html

Textbox
US Government. "Boko Haram in Nigeria Encyclopedia." April 19, 2014. Progressive Management.

Nigerian Flag
Global Panorama, March 2014, accessed on January 16, 2015, https://www.flickr.com/photos/121483302@N02/

Coat of Arms
Federal Republic of Nigeria, *About Nigeria*, accessed December 24, 2014, http://www.nigeria.gov.ng/2012-10-29-11-05-46

Table of Tribes and Religion
Created by Laura Murray with information and data gathered through her research and analysis. See Methodology Section for details on how information was gathered.

Economy Example
Created by Laura Murray with information from:
U.S. Government, Progressive Management, *Boko Haram in Nigeria Encyclopedia,* Washington, DC, April 19, 2014.

Hausa-Fulani

Caused by Fulani Table
Created by Laura Murray with information and data gathered through her research and analysis. See Methodology Section for details on how information was gathered.

Textbox 1
Created by Laura Murray with information gleaned from:
Tony Marinho, "'Our Girls'; Boko Haram/Fulani Wars; Osundare War won with words- People's Poet Laureate," *The Nation*, December 10, 2014, accessed on January 16, 2015, http://thenationonlineng.net/new/girls-boko-haramfulani-wars-osundare-war-won-words-peoples-poet-laureate/

Picture from Shonong Massacre
Provided by an undisclosed Nigeria Correspondent, "Soldiers Join Slaughter of Christians in Nigerian Village, Survivors Say," *Morning Star News,* January 8, 2014, accessed on December 20, 2014, http://morningstarnews.org/2014/01/soldiers-join-slaughter-of-christians-in-nigerian-village-survivors-say/

Boko Haram

Salafi Textbox
Created by Laura Murray

Sharia Law Textbox
Created by Laura Murray with information from:
Toni Johnson and Mohammed Aly Sergie, Council on Foreign Relations, "Islam: Governing Under Sharia," July 25, 2014, accessed on December 12, 2014,
http://www.cfr.org/religion/islam-governing-under-sharia/p8034

Figure 1: Boko Haram Financing
Redrawn for image clarity by Laura Murray. Created By: Beacham Publishing's Terrorism Research & Analysis Consortium (TRAC), *Boko Haram: Coffers and Coffins, A Pandora's Box - the Vast Financing Options for Boko Haram, Support from al Qaeda*, accessed on December 21, 2014,
http://www.trackingterrorism.org/article/new-financing-options-boko-haram/support-al-qaeda

Women Under Sharia Textbox
Created by Laura Murray with information from: David A. "Sharia Law: Unjust & Unconstitutional." iBooks.

Caused by Boko Haram Table
Created by Laura Murray with information and data gathered through her research and analysis. See Methodology Section for details on how information was gathered.

Quran Quote Textbox
Created by Laura Murray with information from:
Quran Surat Muḥammad 47-4, accessed on January 16, 2015,
http://quran.com/47/4

Picture of Jummai Sunday
Provided by an undisclosed Nigeria Correspondent, "Gunmen Kill Christian Widow in Jos, Nigeria Bomb Blasts," *Morning Star News*, December 13, 2014, accessed on January 12, 2015,

http://morningstarnews.org/2014/12/gunmen-kill-christian-widow-in-jos-nigeria-bomb-blasts/

Picture of Hassan
Provided by Stephens Children Home. "Who Did This?" *Stephens Children Home*, November 28, 2014, accessed on January 16, 2015, http://stephensng.org/news-and-events/167-who-did-this

Is It Worth It?

Definition of Sin
Created By Laura Murray with information gleaned from: "How to Become a Christian," Southern Baptist Convention, accessed on January 16, 2015, http://www.sbc.net/knowjesus/theplan.asp

Definition of Trinity
Created by Laura Murray with information gleaned from:
- Apologetics Study Bible
- A formula heard/read but cannot locate person/book (explanation is Laura's thoughts on the formula's representation of Trinity. However, the formula itself is a concept of another person.)

Paul & Silas Textbox
Created by Laura Murray with excerpt from Acts 16 of the Bible

Quran 9:123 Textbox
Created by Laura Murray with excerpt from the Quran

Deception Terms Textbox
Created by Laura Murray with excerpts from:
- Raymond Ibrahim: Islam Translated, "Taqiyya about Taqiyya," Raymond Ibrahim, April 12, 2014, accessed on December 20, 2014,

http://www.raymondibrahim.com/islam/taqiyya-about-taqiyya/
- Raymond Ibrahim, "Tawriya: 'Creative Lying' Advocated in Islam," Gatestone Institute, February 28, 2012, accessed on December 20, 2014, http://www.gatestoneinstitute.org/2898/tawriya-creative-lying-islam

In Memory Of

Christian Deaths by Boko Haram Table
Created by Laura Murray with information and data gathered through her research and analysis. See Methodology Section for details on how information was gathered.

Christian Deaths by Fulani Table
Created by Laura Murray with information and data gathered through her research and analysis. See Methodology Section for details on how information was gathered.

Maps
Security Advisor Clay Murray, Jr. created all maps, for the publication of this book.

Endnotes

[1] UN General Assembly, *Convention on the Prevention and Punishment of the Crime of Genocide*, December 9, 1948, United Nations, Treaty Series, vol. 78,

[2] Federal Republic of Nigeria, *About Nigeria*, accessed December 24, 2014, http://www.nigeria.gov.ng/2012-10-29-11-05-46

[3] "Nigeria," *World Factbook: 2013-14*, U.S. Central Intelligence Agency Office of Public Affairs, accessed December 26, 2014, https://www.cia.gov/library/publications/the-world-factbook/geos/ni.html

[4] U.S. Government, Progressive Management, *Boko Haram in Nigeria Encyclopedia,* Washington, DC, April 19, 2014, 640, Kindle.

[5] Ibid., 546.

[6] Federal Republic of Nigeria, *About Nigeria.*

[7] Ibid.

[8] U.S. Government, *Boko Haram in Nigeria Encyclopedia,* 821, Kindle.

[9] Ibid., 654.

[10] "Nigeria," *World Factbook: 2013-14.*

[11] U.S. Government, *Boko Haram in Nigeria Encyclopedia,* 636, Kindle

[12] Ibid., 683.

[13] Ibid., 696.

[14] "Nigeria," *World Factbook: 2013-14.*

[15] Ibid.

[16] Ibid.

[17] U.S. Government, *Boko Haram in Nigeria Encyclopedia,* 988, Kindle

[18] Marc-Antoine Pérouse de Montclos, *Nigeria Watch Database*, accessed on January 11, 2014
http://www.nigeriawatch.org/index.php?urlaction=evtStat&type=graph

[19] Institute for Economics & Peace, *Global Terrorism Index 2014: Measuring and Understanding the Impact of Terrorism* (November), accessed on December 10, 2014, http://economicsandpeace.org/publications

[20] Guide to Nigeria tourism, local culture and investment opportunities, *Come to Nigeria,* 2010, accessed on November 21, 2014, http://www.cometonigeria.com/about-nigeria/nigerian-people-culture/hausa-and-fulani-people/

[21] U.S. Center for World Mission, *Hausa in Nigeria*, Joshua Project, 2015, accessed on January 16, 2015,
http://joshuaproject.net/people_groups/12070/NI

[22] Ibid.

[23] *Encyclopædia Britannica Online,* s.v. "Fulani," accessed December 27, 2014, http://www.britannica.com/EBchecked/topic/221697/Fulani

[24] Frank Salamone, *Encyclopedia of World Cultures,* s.v. "Fulani," 1996, accessed on January 12, 2015, http://www.encyclopedia.com/doc/1G2-3458001488.html
[25] Ibid.
[26] Ibid.
[27] *Encyclopædia Britannica Online*, s. v. "Fulani."
[28] ASSIST News, "Islamic Extremists Fulani Herdsmen and Boko Haram attacks in Borno Kill at Least 71 Christians in Nigeria Suspected Fulani Herdsmen Slaughter 37 in Plateau State," *Crossmap,* December 1, 2014, accessed on December 20, 1014, http://www.crossmap.com/news/islamic-extremists-boko-haram-attacks-in-borno-kill-at-least-71-christians-in-nigeria-suspected-fulani-herdsmen-slaughter-37-in-plateau-state-7086#ixzz3Mktpq7PV
[29] U.S. Government, *Boko Haram in Nigeria Encyclopedia,* 1070, Kindle.
[30] Ndiameeh Babangida Babreek, "Boko Haram: Is it Northern Hausa/Fulani Muslim Agenda to Depopulate Northern Nigerian Christians and Other Tribes?" *The Nigerian Voice,* October 10, 2014, quote taken from Sir Ahmadu Bello, Premier of Northern Nigeria, in the *The Parrot Newspaper* on October 12, 1960, accessed January 16, 2015, http://www.thenigerianvoice.com/news/159416/1/boko-haram-is-it-northern-hausafula.html
[31] Ibid., quote taken from General Muhammadu Buhari in Kaduna, Nigeria, December 2010.
[32] Ibid., quote taken from Alhaji Lawal Kaita on December 7, 2010.
[33] Allwell Okpi, Hausa-Fulani Politicians Encouraging Boko Haram," *Punch Nigeria Limited,* August 11, 2013, accessed on December 12, 2014, http://www.punchng.com/news/hausa-fulani-politicians-encouraging-boko-haram/
[34] Ibid.
[35] U.S. House of Representatives Committee on Homeland Security, *Boko Haram: Growing Threat to the US Homeland,* 112th Cong., 1st sess. 2011, H Rep. 112-60. Report released on September 13, 2013, accessed on December 19, 2014, http://homeland.house.gov/boko-haram-growing-threat-us-homeland
[36] An undisclosed Nigeria Correspondent, "At Least 205 Christians Killed by Fulani Herdsmen in Benue State, Nigeria," *Morning Star News,* December 17, 2013, accessed on December 20, 2014, http://morningstarnews.org/2013/12/at-least-205-christians-killed-by-fulani-herdsmen-in-benue-state-nigeria/
[37] An undisclosed Nigeria Correspondent, "Two Pastors Among 46 Christians Killed in Kaduna State, Nigeria," *Morning Star News,* September 29, 2014, accessed on December 20, 2014, http://us6.campaign-archive2.com/?u=7ec6d7eb2533a90581f839110&id=ed1794792d&e=4abbc83134
[38] An undisclosed Nigeria Correspondent, "At Least 205 Christians Killed," *Morning Star News,* December 17, 2013.

39 Ibid.
40 An undisclosed Nigeria Correspondent, "More than 76 Christians Killed in Taraba State, Nigeria in Last Four Months," *Morning Star News,* August 6, 2014, accessed on December 17, 2014, http://morningstarnews.org/2014/08/more-than-76-christians-killed-in-taraba-state-nigeria-in-last-four-months/
41 An undisclosed Nigeria Correspondent, "Islamic Extremists in Nigeria Attack Christians at Sunday Worship," *Morning Star News,* January 21, 2014, accessed on January 11, 2015, http://morningstarnews.org/2014/01/islamic-extremists-in-nigeria-attack-christians-at-sunday-worship/
42 Examples are "cattle herders," "Fulani," "cattle rustlers," "Muslim herders," and more.
43 An undisclosed Nigeria Correspondent, "More than 100 Christians Slain as Herdsmen Burn Homes, Church Buildings in Nigeria," *Morning Star News,* March 16, 2014, accessed on January 12, 2015, http://morningstarnews.org/2014/03/more-than-100-christians-slain-as-fulani-herdsmen-burn-homes-church-buildings-in-nigeria/
44 Niyi, "Fulani Herdsmen Invade Taraba Village, Kill 20," *Information Nigeria*, September 15, 2014, accessed on January 16, 2015, http://www.informationng.com/2014/09/fulani-herdsmen-invade-taraba-village-kill-20.html
45 An undisclosed Nigeria Correspondent, "Soldiers Join Slaughter of Christians in Nigerian Village, Survivors Say," *Morning Star News,* January 8, 2014, accessed on December 20, 2014, http://morningstarnews.org/2014/01/soldiers-join-slaughter-of-christians-in-nigerian-village-survivors-say/
46 Daniel (surname not listed), "Soka Forest of Horror: Residents Want Fulani Herdsmen Investigated." *Information Nigeria,* April 6, 2014, accessed on December 20, 2014, http://www.informationng.com/2014/04/soka-forest-of-horror-residents-want-fulani-herdsmen-investigated.html
47 Kingsley Omonobi-Abuja, "Fulani Herdsmen Confess to Membership of Boko Haram," *Vanguard,* April 23, 2014, accessed on December 20, 2014, http://www.vanguardngr.com/2014/04/fulani-herdsmen-confess-membership-boko-haram/
48 Ola Audu, "Boko Haram Abducts 20 Fulani Women, 3 Men near Chibok," *Premium Times Nigeria,* June 10, 2014, accessed on December 22, 2014, http://www.premiumtimesng.com/news/162493-boko-haram-abducts-20-fulani-women-3-men-near-chibok.html
49 Vincent Ehlabhi, "Omeri Denies Abduction of 20 Fulani Women by Boko Haram," *Naij,* June 2014, accessed on December 20, 2014, http://www.naij.com/68131.html
50 ASSIST News, "Islamic Extremists Fulani Herdsmen and Boko Haram attacks in Borno Kill at Least 71 Christians," *Crossmap,* December 1, 2014.
51 Timothy Morgan, "How Boko Haram's Murders and Kidnappings Are Changing Nigeria's Churches," *Christianity Today,* October 16, 2014,

accessed on December 23, 2014, http://www.christianitytoday.com/ct/2014/october-web-only/boko-haram-chibok-hostages-persecution.html?start=2

[52] An undisclosed Nigeria Correspondent, "At Least 205 Christians Killed," *Morning Star News,* December 17, 2013.

[53] Niyi, "Fuani Herdsmen Kill 19, Abduct 15, in Latest Attack on Benue Communities," *Information Nigeria,* March 30, 2014, accessed on November 23, 2014, http://www.informationng.com/2014/03/fulani-herdsmen-kill-19-abduct-15-in-latest-attack-on-benue-communities.html

[54] Daniel (surname not listed), "No Fewer than 100 Killed in Kaduna Village Attack, says CAN," *Information Nigeria,* June 26, 2014, accessed on December 20, 2014, http://www.informationng.com/2014/06/no-fewer-than-100-killed-in-kaduna-village-attack-says-can.html

[55] An undisclosed Nigeria Correspondent, "At Least 205 Christians Killed," *Morning Star News,* December 17, 2013.

[56] An undisclosed Nigeria Correspondent, "Muslim Extremists Kill 31 Christians in Taraba State, Nigeria," *Morning Star News,* October 24, 2014, accessed on December 20, 2014, http://us6.campaign-archive2.com/?u=7ec6d7eb2533a90581f839110&id=fce2237dec&e=4abbc83134

[57] Ibid.
[58] Ibid.
[59] Ibid.
[60] Ibid.
[61] Ibid.

[62] Institute for Economics & Peace, *Global Terrorism Index 2014,* (November), 19.

[63] Alexander Smith, "Nigeria's Boko Haram Violence Now Comparable to ISIS in Iraq," *ABC News,* December 6, 2014, accessed on January 11, 2014, http://www.nbcnews.com/storyline/missing-nigeria-schoolgirls/nigerias-boko-haram-violence-now-comparable-isis-iraq-n260576

[64] Jordan Schachtel, "Boko Haram Now Controls up to Six Times More Territory than ISIS," *Breitbart,* January 2, 2015, accessed on January 12, 2015, http://www.breitbart.com/national-security/2015/01/02/boko-haram-now-controls-up-to-six-times-more-territory-than-isis/

[65] "Boko Haram," Counter Extremist Project, 2014, accessed on December 28, 2014, http://www.counterextremism.com/threat/boko-haram?gclid=CjwKEAiAqrqkBRCep-rKnt_r_lkSJAArVUBcDkR_N1AxTDm3-Oqav7d-tKgv5x5HvUU89IpoXHeiehoCCM7w_wcB

[66] Mohammed Aly Sergie and Toni Johnson, Council on Foreign Relations, *Boko Haram Backgrounder*, December 2011, accessed on December 2014, http://www.cfr.org/nigeria/boko-haram/p25739

[67] Ibid.

[68] Jasmine Oppermen, Terrorism Research and Analysis Consortium, *Boko Haram: Responses to Media Questions*, December 2014, accessed on December 26, 2014,

http://www.trackingterrorism.org.ezproxy1.apus.edu/chatter/trac-insight-boko-haram-responses-media-questions
[69] "Boko Haram," Counter Extremist Project, 2014.
[70] Jacob Zenn, Combating Terrorism Center at West Point, *Boko Haram's International Connections*, January 14, 2014, accessed December 13, 2014, https://www.ctc.usma.edu/posts/boko-harams-international-connections
[71] George Gorman, "Nigerian Taliban leader killed in custody," *The Long War Journal*, July 31, 2009, accessed on January 16, 2015, http://www.longwarjournal.org/archives/2009/07/nigerian_taliban_lea.php
[72] Beacham Publishing's Terrorism Research & Analysis Consortium (TRAC), *Who is the real Abubakar Shekau (aka Abu Muhammad Abubakar Bin Muhammad): Boko Haram's Renegade Warlord*, accessed on January 17 2015, http://www.trackingterrorism.org/article/who-real-abubakar-shekau-aka-abu-muhammad-abubakar-bin-muhammad-boko-harams-renegade-warlord
[73] "Boko Haram," Counter Extremist Project, 2014.
[74] Beacham Publishing's TRAC, *The Triad of Leaders in Boko Haram reflects it's Larger Transnational Aspirations,* accessed on December 21, 2014, http://www.trackingterrorism.org/article/triad-leaders-boko-haram-reflects-its-larger-transnational-aspirations
[75] "Boko Haram," Counter Extremist Project, 2014.
[76] "Nigeria's Boko Haram Leader Profile," BBC, May 9, 2014, accessed on December 28, 2014, http://www.bbc.com/news/world-africa-18020349
[77] Beacham Publishing's TRAC, *The Triad of Leaders in Boko Haram.*
[78] Ibid.
[79] Beacham Publishing's TRAC, *Boko Haram: Coffers and Coffins, A Pandora's Box - the Vast Financing Options for Boko Haram, Support from al Qaeda*, accessed on December 21, 2014, http://www.trackingterrorism.org/article/new-financing-options-boko-haram/support-al-qaeda
[80] Ibid.
[81] Ibid.
[82] "Boko Haram," Counter Extremist Project, 2014.
[83] Beacham Publishing's TRAC, *The Triad of Leaders in Boko Haram.*
[84] START Consortium. "Background Report: Boko Haram." May 2014
[85] "Boko Haram," Counter Extremist Project, 2014.
[86] Amy Pate, Erin Miller, and Michael Jensen, National Consortium for the Study of Terrorism and Responses to Terrorism (START), *Background Report: Boko Haram Recent Attacks*, May 9, 2014, accessed on January 16, 2015, http://www.start.umd.edu/news/background-report-boko-haram-recent-attacks
[87] Amy Pate, et al, START, *Background Report,* May 9, 2014.
[88] Beacham Publishing's TRAC, *The Triad of Leaders in Boko Haram.*
[89] "Boko Haram," Counter Extremist Project, 2014.

[90] "The Soft War: An Undeclared War on Christians in Africa," International Christian Concern, *Persecution* (August 2014): 3-4, accessed on January 16, 2015, http://issuu.com/persecution/docs/2014-08_persecution_newsletter
[91] "We're Going to Kill You," International Christian Concern, *Persecution* (August 2014): 7-8, accessed on January 16, 2015, http://issuu.com/persecution/docs/2014-08_persecution_newsletter
[92] "The Soft War," *Persecution* (August 2014): 3-4.
[93] "Boko Haram," Counter Extremist Project, 2014.
[94] "The Soft War," *Persecution* (August 2014): 3-4.
[95] Ibid.
[96] "Boko Haram," Counter Extremist Project, 2014.
[97] Beacham Publishing's TRAC, *Boko Haram: Coffers and Coffins.*
[98] "Boko Haram," Counter Extremist Project, 2014.
[99] Jacob Zenn and Elizabeth Pearson, "Women, Gender, and the Evolving Tactics of Boko Haram," *Journal of Terrorism Research* Volume 5, Issue 1, accessed on January 16, 2015, http://ojs.st-andrews.ac.uk/index.php/jtr/article/view/828/707
[100] Nina Strochlic, "The New Face of Boko Haram's Terror: Teenage Girls," *Daily Beast,* December 13, 2014, accessed on December 28, 2014, http://www.thedailybeast.com/articles/2014/12/13/the-new-face-of-boko-haram-s-terror-teen-girls.html
[101] "Boko Haram Kills 48 in Nigeria Attack," *ABC News,* November 2014, accessed on December 28, 2014, http://www.abc.net.au/news/2014-11-23/boko-haram-kills-48-in-nigeria-attack-union-leader-says/5912494
[102] "Boko Haram Kills 48 Fish Vendors in Northeast Nigeria," *The National*, November 23, 2014, accessed on January 16, 2015, http://www.thenational.ae/world/africa/boko-haram-kills-48-fish-vendors-in-northeast-nigeria
[103] An undisclosed Nigeria Correspondent, "Two Pastors Among 46 Christians Killed
Morning Star News, September 29, 2014.
[104] "Boko Haram," Counter Extremist Project, 2014.
[105] "Those Terrible Weeks in Their Camp," *Human Rights Watch*, October 27, 2014: 2, accessed on January 16, 2015, http://www.hrw.org/reports/2014/10/27/those-terrible-weeks-their-camp-0
[106] "Boko Haram," Counter Extremist Project, 2014.
[107] Ibid.
[108] Keith Fournier, "Majority of Kidnapped Girls in Nigeria Christians: Is Boko Haram Engaged in a War on Christians?" *Catholic Online,* May 11, 2014, accessed on December 28, 2014, http://www.catholic.org/news/international/africa/story.php?id=55298
[109] Haruna Umar, "Boko Haram Slaughters Mass of Captives in Horrific New Video," *Huffington Post,* December 21, 2014, accessed on December 28,

2014, http://www.huffingtonpost.com/2014/12/21/boko-haram-killings_n_6362030.html

[110] Timothy Morgan, "How Boko Haram's Murders and Kidnappings Are Changing Nigeria's Churches," *Christianity Today,* October 16, 2014, accessed on December 23, 2014, http://www.christianitytoday.com/ct/2014/october-web-only/boko-haram-chibok-hostages-persecution.html?start=2

[111] "Those Terrible Weeks in Their Camp," *Human Rights Watch*, October 27, 2014.

[112] Ibid.

[113] Human Rights Watch, *Nigerian Women Describe Boko Haram Abductions*, Online Video, accessed on December 12, 2014, http://www.hrw.org/news/2014/10/27/nigeria-victims-abductions-tell-their-stories

[114] Ibid.

[115] "Those Terrible Weeks in Their Camp," *Human Rights Watch*, October 27, 2014.

[116] Ibid.

[117] Ibid.

[118] An undisclosed Nigerian Correspondent, "Nigerian Girl Who Escaped Boko Haram Abduction Aches for Schoolmates," *Morning Star News*, June 12, 2014, accessed on January 12, 2015, http://morningstarnews.org/2014/06/nigerian-girl-who-escaped-boko-haram-abduction-aches-for-schoolmates/

[119] Katie Gorka, "Exclusive: Girl Who Escaped Boko Haram Tells Breitbart Her Tale of Survival," *Breitbart News,* September 19, 2014, accessed on December 22, 2014, http://www.breitbart.com/national-security/2014/09/19/exclusive-girl-who-escaped-boko-haram-tells-breitbart-her-tale-of-survival/

[120] "Those Terrible Weeks in Their Camp," *Human Rights Watch*, October 27, 2014.

[121] Committee on Foreign Affairs, *Boko Haram: The Growing Threat to Schoolgirls, Nigeria, and Beyond,* 113th Cong., 2nd sess., 2014.

[122] An undisclosed Nigeria Correspondent, "Two Attempted Murders by Boko Haram Show Islamic Extremist Motives," *Morning Star News,* October 10, 2014, accessed on January 16, 2015, http://morningstarnews.org/2014/10/two-attempted-murders-by-boko-haram-show-islamic-extremist-motives/

[123] "Those Terrible Weeks in Their Camp," *Human Rights Watch*, October 27, 2014.

[124] Ibid.

[125] Maina Maina, "Boko Haram Kills 30, Destroy Houses in Oil-Rich Gajiganna," *Daily Post,* December 14, 2014, accessed on December 21, 2014, http://dailypost.ng/2014/12/14/boko-haram-kills-30-destroy-houses-oil-rich-gajiganna/

[126] Molly Kilete, "Boko Haram Grave Digger's Horror," *The Sun,* November 26, 2014, accessed on December 14, 2014, http://sunnewsonline.com/new/?p=92702

[127] An undisclosed Nigeria Correspondent, "Gunmen Kill Christian Widow in Jos, Nigeria Bomb Blasts," *Morning Star News*, December 13, 2014, accessed on January 12, 2015, http://morningstarnews.org/2014/12/gunmen-kill-christian-widow-in-jos-nigeria-bomb-blasts/

[128] "Those Terrible Weeks in Their Camp," *Human Rights Watch*, October 27, 2014.

[129] An undisclosed Nigeria Correspondent, "Two Attempted Murders by Boko Haram," *Morning Star News,* October 10, 2014.

[130] House Subcommittee on Africa, Global Health, Global Human Rights, and International Organizations and the Subcommittee on Terrorism, Non-proliferation and Trade, *Congressional Testimony of Habila Adamu on the Continuing Threat of Boko Haram,* 113th Cong., 1st sess., 2013.

[131] "Who Did This?" *Stephens Children Home*, November 28, 2014, accessed on January 16, 2015, http://stephensng.org/news-and-events/167-who-did-this

[132] Kareem Haruna, "Boko Haram: Residents in Captured Borno Communities Pay Allegiance to Chadian Mercenaries," *Leadership Newspapers,* December 15, 2014, accessed on December 28, 2014, http://leadership.ng/news/395265/boko-haram-residents-captured-borno-communities-pays-allegiance-chadian-mercenaries

[133] Ibid.

[134] Wale Odunsi, "Army Uncovers Plan by Boko Haram to Invade Five States," *Daily Post Nigeria,* December 12, 2014, accessed on December 28, 2014, http://dailypost.ng/2014/12/12/army-uncovers-plan-boko-haram-invade-five-states/

[135] "Nigeria 2014 Sees Bloodier, Emboldened Boko Haram," *World Bulletin,* December 22, 2014, accessed on January 16, 2015, http://www.worldbulletin.net/world/151389/nigeria-2014-sees-bloodier-emboldened-boko-haram

[136] Associated Press, "Nigeria: 11 Parents of Kidnapped Schoolgirls Killed in Militant Attack," *First Post*, July 22, 2014, accessed on January 16, 2015, http://www.firstpost.com/world/nigeria-11-parents-of-kidnapped-schoolgirls-killed-in-attack-1629215.html

[137] "Those Terrible Weeks in Their Camp," *Human Rights Watch*, October 27, 2014: 5

[138] Adelani Adepegba and Temitayo Famutimi, "Chibok girls: Police stop protesters in Abuja," *Punch Nigeria Limited*, December 26, 2014, accessed on January 16, 2015, http://www.punchng.com/news/chibok-girls-police-stop-protesters-in-abuja/

[139] Vincent Ehiabhi, "EU Assists Boko Haram Displaced Victims with More Funds," *Naij,* December 2014, accessed on January 16, 2015, http://www.naij.com/331867-eu-assists-boko-haram-displaced-victims-with-more-funds.html

[140] "Nigeria: Examining Boko Haram," KVUE-TV News Online, November 18, 2014, accessed on January 12, 2015, http://www.kvue.com/story/news/world/stratfor/2014/11/10/nigeria-examining-boko-haram/18813407/
[141] "Those Terrible Weeks in Their Camp," *Human Rights Watch*, October 27, 2014: 41.
[142] U.S. Government, *Boko Haram in Nigeria Encyclopedia,* 5763, Kindle.
[143] Ibid., 5777.
[144] Eric Schmitt, "With Schoolgirls Taken by Boko Haram Still missing, US-Nigeria Ties Falter," *New York Times,* December 31, 2014, accessed on January 11, 2015, http://www.nytimes.com/2015/01/01/world/with-schoolgirls-still-missing-fragile-us-nigeria-ties-falter.html?_r=0
[145] Ibid.
[146] Timothy Morgan, "How Boko Haram's Murders and Kidnappings Are Changing Nigeria's Churches," *Christianity Today,* October 16, 2014.
[147] Jeff Schogol and Joe Gould, "Nigeria ends US mission to Counter Boko Haram," *Military Times,* December 1, 2014, accessed on December 30, 2014, http://www.militarytimes.com/story/military/2014/12/01/nigeria-ends-us-mission-counter-boko-haram/19743581/
[148] Adelani Adepegba and Temitayo Famutimi, "Chibok girls," *Punch Nigeria Limited*, December 26, 2014. http://www.punchng.com/news/chibok-girls-police-stop-protesters-in-abuja/
[149] Monica Mark, "When They Took the Girls, Our Government Went Under," *The Guardian,* December 28, 2014, accessed on December 28, 2014, http://www.theguardian.com/world/2014/dec/28/obiageli-ezekwesili-bring-back-our-girls-boko-haram-school-kidnapping
[150] Schmitt, Eric. *New York Times.* "With Schoolgirls Taken by Boko Haram Stil Missing, US-Nigeria Ties Falter." http://www.nytimes.com/2015/01/01/world/with-schoolgirls-still-missing-fragile-us-nigeria-ties-falter.html?_r=1 Last Accessed January 12, 2015
[151] Eric Schmitt, "With Schoolgirls Taken by Boko Haram Still missing," *New York Times,* December 31, 2014.
[152] Whitney Eulich, "Chibok Girls: Police Stop Protesters in Abuja," *Christian Science Monitor,* December 18, 2014, accessed on December 28, 2014, http://www.csmonitor.com/World/Security-Watch/terrorism-security/2014/1218/Nigeria-sentences-mutinous-soldiers-to-death-as-Boko-Haram-stages-major-attack-video
[153] Acts 16:16-40, available online at https://www.biblegateway.com/passage/?search=Acts%2016%3A16-40
[154] Ahmad ibn Naqib al-Misri, *The Reliance of the Traveller*, translated by Nuh Ha Mim Keller, (Amana Publications, section r8.2, 1997) 745, from Warner MacKenzie, "Understanding Taqiyya — Islamic Principle of Lying for the Sake of Allah," *Islam Watch,* April 30, 2007, accessed on January 16, 2015, http://www.islam-watch.org/Warner/Taqiyya-Islamic-Principle-Lying-for-Allah.htm

[155] Raymond Ibrahim: Islam Translated, "Taqiyya about Taqiyya," Raymond Ibrahim, April 12, 2014, accessed on December 20, 2014, http://www.raymondibrahim.com/islam/taqiyya-about-taqiyya/
[156] Ibid.
[157] Timothy Morgan, "How Boko Haram's Murders and Kidnappings Are Changing Nigeria's Churches," *Christianity Today,* October 16, 2014.